The Original Maccabees Bible
With Psalm 151

Published By:
Research Associates School Times Publications

Frontline Distribution International Inc.
and
Miguel Lorne Publishers, Jamaica
Chicago • Jamaica • London • Republic of Trinidad and Tobago

Published by:

Research Associates School Times Publications
and
Frontline Distribution Int'l Inc.
5206 S. Harper Ave.
Chicago, IL 60615
Tel: (773) 288-7718
Fax: ((773) 288-7528
Email: info@frontlinebooks.net/com

First Published 2000
Second Reprint 2002
Third Reprint 2007

The Original Maccabees Bible - The Book Of Maccabees
Introduction © Rev. Roderick M. McLean, Ph.D.
First Published Unknown

ISBN: 0-94839-046-8

Library Of Congress Catalog in Publication Data 98-66859

MACCABEES BIBLE

Contents

THE BOOKS OF THE MACCABEES

The first and second books of the Maccabees were part of the Latin Bible. In the Protestant Church they were not included amongst the canonical books. But they are part of the Apocrypha, that is, books withdrawn from holy use. The Jewish standard of judgement was accepted, and they did not form part of the Hebrew Bible. In the Thirty-nine Articles of the Anglican Church it is said of the Apocrypha:'Other books the Church doth read for examples of life and instruction of manners; but does not apply them to establish any doctrine'. They were not considered to be inspired like Holy Writ. But the English poet Coleridge wrote of the books of the Maccabees:'They are so inspiring as to be inspired'.

The two books record the heroic struggle of the Jewish people for religious freedom in the second century before the Christian Era, when the little nation stood against the might of the Seleucid Empire. That struggle marked one of the turning points in the history of civilization. Through it Hebraism and the Jewish religion became conscious of their moral strength, and could hold their own against the dominant Hellenism.

The deeds of the Maccabean brothers have received in our day a fresh significance, as has the festival of Chanuka which celebrates their triumph. They reflect the spirit of national revival which has culminated in the foundation of the State of Israel. In the Jewish Calendar of feasts and fasts Chanuka has a fresh popularity greater than that accorded to the major festivals; for we are living again through an age of destiny of the Jewish people such as the Books of the Maccabees commemorate.

The first Maccabees, in particular, should be read by all who are concerned with the Jewish renascence. It is a simple, direct, historical narrative of the forty years' struggle, from 175 to 135 B.C., from the accession of Antiochus IV (Epiphanes) to the death of Simon, the youngest of the Maccabean brothers. It was written originally in Hebrew; but the Hebrew text has been lost, and our English book is a translation from the Greek. The hero is Judas Maccabaus. It is a striking feature that the name of God never occurs, though a sense of divine providence is a pervading theme. The second book of the Maccabees covers part of the same period of history, but the record is more rhetorical and ornate. It was originally written by a Hellenized Jew of Cyrene. The name of God occurs frequently, and the purpose of the book was to impress the large Jewish community in Egypt with the significance of the festival of Chanuka.

Two other books in the Apocrypha bear the name of the Maccabees, but are very different in character. The one is a work of moralizing fiction, which tells how King Ptolemy of Egypt, after his defeat by Antiochus the Great of Syria in 217 B.C., conceived the idea of entering the Holy of Holies in the Temple of Jerusalem; but, after the High-Priest Simon had prayed to avert the desecration, the King was smitten with paralysis. He sought later to wreak his vengeance on the Jews in Alexandria, but again a miracle prevented him. Elephants made drunk and let loose on the Jews in the racecourse turned and trampled down the royal forces. The book was written in Greek by an Alexandrian Jew, and neither in substance nor in style is it distinguished. A strange fate preserved it for posterity out of many of the kind.

The fourth book of the Maccabees is a philosophical dissertation in the form of a sermon, which expounds the supremacy of pious reason over the passions, and draws its examples from the stories of the Maccabean martyrs, Eleazar, the aged priest, and the seven children who, in the presence of their mother, chose death rather than deny their belief in the one God. Here Judaism is tinged with the influence of the Stoic philosophy; and the book marks that combination of Hebraism and a purer Hellenism which was one of the outcomes of the struggle, and prepared the way for the mission of the Jew to the Gentile.

PREFACE

The Maccabees is a masterpiece of literary and theological import. It savors of the legendary in certain aspects of its historical accounts. However, it borders on a historical narration that is somewhat romanticized to encourage, stimulate and edify the faithful, and to present to outsiders a perspective of a "special people". Although the authors did not project any heroes or heroines as a specific models for our day, they relied on the biblical figures as archetypals for the faithful and thus the holy books as a source of encouragement and an instrument of the virtues of loyalty and obedience to the Law, and ritual and festival observances.

The primary thrust of this work presents martyrdom as paradigmatic materials for philosophical exercise on the subject of devout's reason mastery over passion. It relies on the framework of Greek thought and platonic ideas, and celebrates the virtues of chastity and familial piety.

A recurring theme throughout this work is that reason does not eradicate, it only controls or directs passion. It also states that we must lead our lives in accordance with divine law, and that under no circumstances whatever do we deem it right to transgress the law.

One of the most significant contributions in these pages is the development of the notion that the suffering and death of the martyred righteous had redemptive efficacy for all Israel, and secured God's grace and pardon for his people, and that loyal obedience to the revealed will of God will win spiritual victory over death. There is great emphasis, not on the individual, but on the people of God as a whole.

In the history and development of religious thought and practice this work of the Maccabees stands as a creative paradigm for stimulating and motivating the faithful to pursue rigorously spiritual insights to address the alienation and despair experienced by those searching for an anchor in the storms of life. It provides a bulwark for those experiencing oppression and persecution. It challenges the faithful to a higher calling and level of spiritual discipline and exercise in one's daily life. But even more importantly, it is not simply the individual renewal and atonement that are at stake , but the nation, the people of God, and in the words of the celebrated poet Henry Miller ...

> Life moves on, whether we act as
> cowards or heroes.
> Life has no other
> discipline to impose,
> if we would but realize it,
> than to accept life unquestioningly.
> Everything we shut our eyes to,
> Everything we run away from,
> Everything we deny,
> Denigrate or despise,
> serve to defeat us in the end.
> What seems nasty, painful, evil
> can become a source of beauty, joy,
> and strength,
> if faced with an open mind.
> Every moment is a golden one
> for him who has the vision
> to recognize it as such.

I heartily recommend this masterpiece as excellent reading, and as a religious manual for the faithful.

Rev. Roderick M. McLean, Ph.d

1 MACCABEES

(FIRST CENTURY A.D.)

A NEW TRANSLATION AND INTRODUCTION
BY H. ANDERSON

And it came to pass, after that Alexander the Macedonian, the son of Philip, who came out of the land of Chittim, and smote Darius king of the Persians and Medes, it came to pass, after he had smitten him, that he reigned in his stead, in former time, over Greece. And he fought many battles, and won many strongholds, and slew the kings of the earth, and went through to the ends of the earth, and took spoils of a multitude of nations. And the earth was quiet before him, and he was exalted, and his heart was lifted up, and he gathered together an exceeding strong host, and ruled over countries and nations and principalities, and they became tributary unto him. And after these things he fell sick, and perceived that he should die. And he called his servants, which were honourable, which had been brought up with him from his youth, and he divided unto them his kingdom, while he was yet alive. And Alexander reigned twelve years, and he died. And his servants bare rule, each one in his place. And they did all put diadems upon themselves after that he was dead, and so did their sons after them many years: and they multiplied evils in the earth.

And there came forth out of them a sinful root Antiochus Epiphanes, son of Antiochus the king, who had been a hostage at Rome, and he reigned in the hundred and thirty and seventh year of the kingdom of the Greeks.

In those days came there forth out of Israel transgressors of the law, and persuaded many, saying, Let us go and make a covenant with the Gentiles that are round about us: for since we were parted from them many evils have befallen us And the saying was good in their eyes. And certain of the people were forward herein and went to the king, and he gave them license to do after the ordinances of the Gentiles. And they built a place of exercise in Jerusalem according to the laws of the Gentiles; and they made themselves uncircumcised, and forsook the holy covenant, and joined themselves to the Gentiles, and sold themselves to do evil.

And the kingdom was well ordered in the sight of Antiochus, and he thought to reign over Egypt, that he might reign over the two kingdoms. And he entered into Egypt with a great multitude, with chariots, and with elephants, and with horsemen, and with a great navy; and he made war against Ptolemy king of Egypt; and Ptolemy was put to shame before him, and fled; and many fell wounded to death. And they got possession of the strong cities in the land of Egypt; and he took the spoils of Egypt.

And Antiochus, after that he had smitten Egypt, returned in the hundred and forty and third year, and went up against Israel and Jerusalem with a great multitude, and entered presumptuously into the sanctuary, and took the golden altar, and the candlestick of the light, and all that pertained thereto, and the table of the shewbread, and the cups to pour withal, and the bowls, and the golden censers, and the veil, and the crowns, and the adorning of gold which was on the face of the temple, and he scaled it all off. And he took the silver and the gold and the precious vessels; and he took the hidden treasures which he found. And when he had taken all, he went away into his own land, and he made a great slaughter, and spake very presumptuously. And there came great mourning upon Israel, in every place where they were; and the rulers and elders groaned, the virgins and young men were made feeble, and the beauty of the women was changed. Every bridegroom took up lamentation, she that sat in the marriage chamber was in heaviness. And the land was moved for the inhabitants thereof, and all the house of Jacob was clothed with shame.

And after two full years the king sent a chief collector of tribute unto the cities of Judah, and he came unto Jerusalem with a great multitude. And he spake words of peace unto them in subtility, and they gave him credence: and he fell upon the city suddenly, and smote it very sore, and destroyed much people out of Israel. And he took the spoils of the city, and set it on fire, and pulled down the houses thereof and the walls thereof on every side. And they led captive the women and the children, and the cattle they took in possession. And they builded the city of David with a great and strong wall, with strong towers, and it became unto them a citadel. And they put there a sinful nation, transgressors of the law, and they strengthened themselves therein. And they stored up arms and victuals, and gathering together the spoils of Jerusalem, they laid them up there, and they became a sore snare: and it became a place to lie in wait in against the sanctuary, and an evil adversary to Israel continually. And they shed innocent blood on every side of the sanctuary, and defiled the sanctuary. And the inhabitants of Jerusalem fled because of them; and she became a habitation of strangers, and she became strange to them that were born in her, and her children forsook her. Her sanctuary was laid waste like a wilderness, her feasts were turned into mourning, her sabbaths into reproach, her honour into contempt. According to her glory, so was her dishonor multiplied, and her high estate was turned into mourning.

And king Antiochus wrote to his whole kingdom, that all should be one people, and that each should forsake his own laws. And all the nations agreed according to the word of the king; and many of Israel consented to his worship, and sacrificed to the idols, and profaned the sabbath. And the king sent letters by the hand of messengers Unto Jerusalem and the cities of Judah, that they should follow laws strange to the land, and should forbid whole burnt offerings and sacrifice and drink offerings in the sanctuary; and should profane the sabbaths and feasts, and pollute the sanctuary and them that were holy; that they should build altars, and temples, and shrines for idols, and should sacrifice swine's flesh and unclean beasts: and that they should leave their sons uncircumcised, that they should make their souls abominable with all manner of uncleanness and profanation; so that they might forget the law, and change all the ordinances. And whosoever shall not do according to the word of the king, he shall die. According to all these words wrote he to his whole kingdom; and he appointed overseers over all the people, and he commanded the cities of Judah to sacrifice, city by city. And from the people were gathered together unto them many, every one that had forsaken the law; and they did evil things in the land; and they made Israel to hide themselves in every place of refuge which they had.

And on the fifteenth day of Chislev, in the hundred and forty and fifth year, they builded an abomination of desolation upon the altar, and in the cities of Judah on every side they builded idol altars. And at the doors of the houses and in the streets they burnt incense. And they rent in pieces the books of the law which they found, and set them on fire. And wheresoever was found with any a book of the covenant, and if any consented to the law, the king's sentence delivered him to death. Thus did they in their might unto Israel, to those that were found month by month in the cities. And on the five and twentieth day of the month they sacrificed upon the idol altar, which was upon the altar of God. And the women that had circumcised their children they put to death according to the commandment. And they hanged their babes about their necks, and destroyed their houses, and them that had circumcised them. And many in Israel were fully resolved and confirmed in themselves not to eat unclean things. And they chose to die, that they might not be defiled with the meats, and that they might not profane the holy covenant: and they died. And there came exceeding great wrath upon Israel.

CHAPTER II

In those days rose up Mattathias the son of John, the son of Simeon, a priest of the sons of Joarib, from Jerusalem; and he dwelt at Modin. And he had five sons, John, who was surnamed Gaddis; Simon, who was called Thassi; Judas, who was called Maccabaeus; Eleazar, who was called Avaran; Jonathan, who was called Apphus.

And he saw the blasphemies that were committed in Judah and in Jerusalem, and he said,

Woe is me! wherefore was I born to see the destruction of my people, and the destruction of the holy city, and to dwell there, when it was given into the hand of the enemy, the sanctuary into the hand of aliens ? Her temple is become as a man that was glorious: her vessels of glory are carried away into captivity, her infants are slain in her streets, her young men with the sword of the enemy. What nation hath not inherited her palaces, and gotten possession of her spoils ? her adorning is all taken away; instead of a free woman she is become a bond woman: and, behold, our holy things and our beauty and our glory are laid waste, and the Gentiles have profaned them. Wherefore should we live any longer ?

And Mattathias and his sons rent their clothes, and put on sackcloth, and mourned exceedingly.

And the king's officers, that were enforcing the apostasy, came into the city Modin to sacrifice. And many of Israel came unto them, and Mattathias and his sons were gathered together. And the king's officers answered and spake to Mattathias, saying, Thou art a ruler and an honourable and great man in this city, and strengthened with sons and brethren: now therefore come thou first and do the commandment of the king, as all nations have done, and the men of Judah, and they that remain in Jerusalem: and thou and thy house shall be in the number of the king's Friends, and thou and thy sons shall be honoured with silver and gold and many gifts. And Mattathias answered and said with a loud voice, If all the nations that are in the house of the king's dominion hearken unto him, to fall away each one from the worship of his fathers, and have made choice to follow his commandments, yet will I and my sons and my brethren walk in the covenant of our fathers. Heaven forbid that we should forsake the law and the ordinances. We will not hearken to the king's words, to go aside from our worship, on the right hand, or on the left.

And when he had left speaking these words, there came a Jew in the sight of all to sacrifice on the altar which was at Modin, according to the king's commandment. And Mattathias saw it, and his zeal was kindled, and his reins trembled, and he shewed forth his wrath according to judgement, and ran, and slew him upon the altar. And the king's officer, who compelled men to sacrifice, he killed at that time, and pulled down the altar. And he was zealous for the law, even as Phinehas did unto Zimri the son of Salu. And Mattathias cried out in the city with a loud voice, saying, Whosoever is zealous for the law, and maintaineth the covenant, let him come forth after me. And he and his sons fled into the mountains, and forsook all that they had in the city.

Then many that sought after justice and judgement went down into the wilderness, to dwell there, they, and their sons, and their wives, and their cattle; because evils were multiplied upon them. And it was told the king's officers, and the forces that were in Jerusalem, the city of David, that certain men, who had broken the king's commandment, were gone down into the secret places in the wilderness; and many pursued after them, and having overtaken them, they encamped against them, and set the battle in array against them on the sabbath day. And they said unto them, Thus far. Come forth, and do according to the word of the king, and ye shall live. And they said, We will not come forth, neither will we do the word of the king, to profane the sabbath day. And they hasted to give them battle. And they answered them not, neither cast they a stone at them, nor stopped up the secret places, saying, Let us die all in our innocency: heaven and earth witness over us, that ye put us to death without trial. And they rose up against them in battle on the sabbath, and they died, they and their wives and their children, and their cattle, to the number of a thousand souls.

And Mattathias and his friends knew it, and they mourned over them exceedingly. And one said to another, If we all do as our brethren have done, and fight not against the Gentiles for our lives and our ordinances, they will now quickly destroy us from off the earth. And they took counsel on that day, saying, Whosoever shall come against us to battle on the sabbath day, let us fight against him, and we shall in no wise all die, as our brethren died in the secret places. Then were gathered together unto them a company of Hasidaeans, mighty men of Israel, every one that offered himself willingly for the law. And all they that fled from the evils were added to them, and became a stay unto them. And they mustered a host, and smote sinners in their anger, and lawless men in their wrath: and the rest fled to the Gentiles for safety. And Mattathias and his friends went round about, and pulled down the altars; and they circumcised by force the children that were uncircumcised, as many as they found in the coasts of Israel. And they pursued after the sons of pride, and the work prospered in their hand. And they rescued the law out of the hand of the Gentiles, and out the hand of the kings, neither suffered they the sinner to triumph.

And the days of Mattathias drew near that he should die, and he said unto his sons,

Now have pride and rebuke gotten strength, and a season of overthrow, and wrath of indignation. And now, my children, be ye zealous for the law, and give your lives for the covenant of your fathers. And call to remembrance the deeds of our fathers which they did in their generations; and receive great glory and an everlasting name. Was not Abraham found faithful in temptation, and it was reckoned unto him for righteousness ? Joseph in the time of his distress kept the commandment, and became lord of Egypt. Phinehas our father, for that he was zealous exceedingly, obtained the covenant of an everlasting priesthood. Joshua for fulfilling the word became a judge in Israel. Caleb for bearing witness in the congregation obtained a heritage in the land. David for being merciful inherited the throne of a kingdom for ever and ever. Elijah, for that he was exceeding zealous for the law, was taken up into heaven. Hananiah, Azariah, Mishael, believed, and were saved out of the flame. Daniel for his innocency was delivered from the mouth of lions. And thus consider ye from generation to generation, that none that put their trust in him shall want for strength. And be not afraid of the words of a sinful man; for his glory shall be dung and worms. To-day he shall be lifted up, and to-morrow he shall in no wise be found, because he is returned unto his dust, and his thought is perished. And ye, my children, be strong, and shew yourselves men in behalf of the law; for therein shall ye obtain glory. And, behold, Simon your brother, I know that he is a man of counsel; give ear unto him always: he shall be a father unto you. And Judas Maccabaeus, he hath been strong and mighty from his youth: he shall be your captain, and shall fight the battle of the people. And take ye unto you all the doers of the law, and avenge the wrong of your people. Render a recompense to the Gentiles, and take heed to the commandments of the law.

And he blessed them, and was gathered to his fathers. And he died in the hundred and forty and sixth year, and his sons buried him in the sepulchres of his fathers at Modin, and all Israel made great lamentation for him.

CHAPTER 111

And his son Judas, who was called Maccabaeus, rose up in his stead. And all his brethren helped him, and so did all they that clave unto his father, and they fought with gladness the battle of Israel. And he gat his people great glory, and put on a breastplate as a giant, and girt his warlike harness about him, and set battles in array, protecting the army with his sword. And he was like a lion in his deeds, and as a lion's whelp roaring for prey. And he pursued the lawless, seeking them out, and he burnt up those that troubled his people. And the lawless shrunk for fear of him, and all the workers of lawlessness were sore troubled, and salvation prospered in his hand. And he angered many kings, and made Jacob glad with his acts, and his memorial is blessed for ever. And he went about among the cities of Judah, and destroyed the ungodly out of the land, and turned away wrath from Israel: and he was renowned unto the utmost part of the earth, and he gathered together such as were ready to perish.

And Apollonius gathered the Gentiles together, and a great host from Samaria, to fight against Israel. And Judas perceived it, and he went forth to meet him, and smote him, and slew him: and many fell wounded to death, and the rest fled. And they took their spoils, and Judas took the sword of Apollonius, and therewith he fought all his days.

And Seron, the commander of the host of Syria, heard say that Judas had gathered a gathering and a congregation of faithful men with him, and such as went out to war; and he said, I will make myself a name and get me glory in the kingdom; and I will fight against Judas and them that are with him, that set at nought the word of the king. And there went up with him also a mighty army of the ungodly to help him, to take vengeance on the children of Israel.

And he came near unto the going up of Bethhoron, and Judas went forth to meet him with a small company. But when they saw the army coming to meet them, they said unto Judas, What ? shall we be able, being a small company, to fight against so great and strong a multitude? and we for our part are faint, having tasted no food this day. And Judas said, It is an easy thing for many to be shut up in the hands of a few; and with heaven it is all one, to save by many or by few: for victory in battle standeth not in the multitude of a host; but strength is from heaven. They come unto us in fullness of insolence and lawlessness, to destroy us and our wives and our children, for to spoil us: but we fight for our lives and our laws. And he himself will discomfit them before our face: but as for you, be ye not afraid of them.

Now when he had left off speaking, he leapt suddenly upon them, and Seron and his army were discomfited before him. And they pursued them in the going down of Bethhoron unto the plain, and there fell of them about eight hundred men; but the residue fled into the land of the Philistines.

And the fear of Judas and his brethren, and the dread of them, began to fall upon the nations round about them: and his name came near even unto the king, and every nation told of the battles of Judas.

But when king Antiochus heard these words, he was full of indignation: and he sent and gathered together all the forces of his realm, an exceeding strong army. And he opened his treasury, and gave his forces pay for a year, and commanded them to be ready for every need. And he saw that the money failed from his treasures, and that the tributes of the country were small, because of the dissension and plague which he had brought upon the land, to the end that he might take away the laws which had been from the first days; and he feared that he should not have enough as at other times for the charges and the gifts which he gave aforetime with a liberal hand, and he abounded above the kings that were before him. And he was exceedingly perplexed in his mind, and he determined to go into Persia, and to take the tributes of the countries, and to gather much money. And he left Lysias, an honourable man, and one of the seed royal, to be over the affairs of the king from the river Euphrates unto the borders of Egypt, and to bring up his son Antiochus until he came again. And he delivered unto him the half of his forces, and the elephants, and gave him charge of all the things that he would have done, and concerning them that dwelt in Judea and in Jerusalem, that he should send a host against them, to root out and destroy the strength of Israel, and the remnant of Jerusalem, and to take away their memorial from the place; and that he should make strangers to dwell in all their coasts, and should divide their land to them by lot. And the king took the half that remained of the forces, and removed from Antioch, from his royal city, the hundred and forty and seventh year; and he passed over the river Euphrates, and went through the upper countries.

And Lysias chose Ptolemy the son of Dorymenes, and Nicanor, Gorgias, mighty men of the king's Friends; and with them he sent forty thousand footmen and seven thousand horse, to go into the land of Judah, and to destroy it, according to the word of the king. And they removed with all their host, and came and pitched near unto Emmaus in the plain country. And the merchants of the country heard the fame of them, and took silver and gold exceeding much, with fetters, and came into the camp to take the children of Israel for servants: and there were added unto them the forces of Syria and of the land of the Philistines.

And Judas and his brethren saw that evils were multiplied, and that the forces were encamping in their borders; and they took knowledge of the king's words which he had commanded, to destroy the people and make an end of them; and they said each man to his neighbour, Let us raise up the ruin of our people, and let us fight for our people and the holy place. And the congregation was gathered together, that they might be ready for battle, and that they might pray, and ask for mercy and compassion. And Jerusalem was without inhabitant as a wilderness, there was none of her offspring that went in or went out; and the sanctuary was trodden down, and the sons of strangers were in the citadel, the Gentiles lodged therein; and joy was taken away from Jacob, and the pipe and the harp ceased. And they gathered themselves together, and came to Mizpeh, over against Jerusalem; for in Mizpeh was there a place of prayer aforetime for Israel. And they fasted that day, and put on sackcloth, and put ashes upon their heads, and rent their clothes, and laid open the book of the law, concerning which the Gentiles were wont to inquire, seeking the likenesses of their idols. And they brought the priests' garments, and the firstfruits, and the tithes: and they stirred up the Nazirites, who had accomplished their days. And they cried aloud toward heaven, saying, What shall we do with these men, and whither shall we carry them away ? And thy holy place is trodden down and profaned, and thy priests are in heaviness and brought low. And, behold, the Gentiles are assembled together against us to destroy us: thou knowest what things they imagine against us. How shall we be able to stand before them, except thou be our help? And they sounded with the trumpets, and cried with a loud voice.

And after this Judas appointed leaders of the people, captains of thousands, and captains of hundreds, and captains of fifties, and captains of tens: And he said to them that were building houses, and were betrothing wives, and were planting vineyards, and were fearful, that they should return, each man to his own house, according to the law. And the army removed, and encamped upon the south side of Emmaus. And Judas said, Gird yourselves, and be valiant men, and be in readiness against the morning, that ye may fight with these Gentiles, that are assembled together against us to destroy us, and our holy place: for it is better for us to die in battle, than to look upon the evils of our nation and the holy place. Nevertheless, as may be the will in heaven, so shall he do.

CHAPTER IV

And Gorgias took five thousand footmen, and a thousand chosen horse, and the army removed by night, that it might fall upon the army of the Jews and smite them suddenly: and the men of the citadel were his guides. And Judas heard thereof, and removed, he and the valiant men, that he might smite the king's host which was at Emmaus, while as yet the forces were dispersed from the camp. And Gorgias came into the camp of Judas by night, and found no man: and be sought them in the mountains; for he said, These men flee from us. And as soon as it was day, Judas appeared in the plain with three thousand men: howbeit they had not armour nor swords to their minds. And they saw the camp on the Gentiles strong and fortified, and horsemen compassing it around about; and these were expert in war. And Judas said to the men that were with him, Fear ye not their multitude, neither be ye afraid of their onset. Remember how our fathers were saved in the Red sea, when Pharaoh pursued them with a host. And now let us cry unto heaven, if he will have us, and will remember the covenant of our fathers, and destroy this army before our face to-day: and all the Gentiles shall know that there is one who redeemeth and saveth Israel. And the strangers lifted up their eyes, and saw them coming over against them: and they went out of the camp to battle. And they that were with Judas sounded their trumpets, and joined battle, and the Gentiles were discomfited, and fled into the plain. But all the hindmost fell by the sword: and they pursued them unto Gazara, and unto the plains of Idumaea and Azotus and Jamnia, and there fell of them about three thousand men. And Judas and his host returned from pursuing after them, and he said unto the people, Be not greedy of the spoils, inasmuch as there is a battle before us; and Gorgias and his host are nigh unto us in the mountain. But stand ye now against our enemies, and fight against them, and afterwards take the spoils with boldness. While Judas was yet making an end of these words, there appeared a part of them looking out from the mountain: and they saw that their host had been put to flight, and that the Jews were burning the camp; for the smoke that was seen declared what was done. But when they perceived these things, they were sore afraid; and perceiving also the army of Judas in the plain ready for battle, they fled all of them into the land of the Philistines. And Judas returned to spoil the camp, and they got much gold, and silver, and blue, and sea purple, and great riches. And they returned home, and sang a song of thanksgiving and gave praise unto heaven; because his mercy is good, because his mercy endureth for ever. And Israel had a great deliverance that day.

But the strangers, as many as had escaped, came

and told Lysias all the things that had happened: but when he heard thereof, he was confounded and discouraged, because neither had such things as he would been done unto Israel, nor had such things as the king commanded him come to pass.

And in the next year he gathered together threescore thousand chosen footmen, and five thousand horse, that he might subdue them. And they came into Idumaea, and encamped at Bethsura; and Judas met them with ten thousand men. And he saw that the army was strong, and he prayed and said,

Blessed art thou, O Saviour of Israel, who didst quell the onset of the mighty man by the hand of thy servant David, and didst deliver the army of the Philistines into the hands of Jonathan the son of Saul, and of his armourbearer: shut up this army in the hand of thy people Israel, and let them be ashamed for their host and their horsemen: give them faintness of heart, and cause the boldness of their strength to melt away, and let them quake at their destruction: cast them down with the sword of them that love thee, and let all that know thy name praise thee with thanksgiving.

And they joined battle; and there fell of the army of Lysias about five thousand men and they fell down over against them. But when Lysias saw that his array was put to flight, and the boldness that had come upon them that were with Judas, and how they were ready either to live or to die nobly, he removed to Antioch, and gathered together hired soldiers, that he might come again into Judaea with even a greater company.

But Judas and his bretheren said, Behold, our enemies are discomfited: let us go up to cleanse the holy place, and to dedicate it afresh. And all the army was gathered together, and they went up unto mount Sion. And they saw the sanctuary laid desolate, and the altar profaned, and the gates burned up, and shrubs growing in the courts as in a forest or as on one of the mountains, and the priests' chambers pulled down; and they rent their clothes, and made great lamentation, and put ashes upon their heads, and fell on their faces to the ground, and blew with the solemn trumpets, and cried toward heaven. Then Judas appointed certain men to fight against those that were in the citadel, until he should have cleansed the holy place.

And he chose blameless priests, such as had pleasure in the law: and they cleansed the holy place, and bare out the stones of defilement into an unclean place. And they took counsel concerning the altar of burnt offerings, which had been profaned, what they should do with it: and there came into their mind a good counsel, that they should pull it down, lest it should be a reproach to them, because the Gentiles had defiled it: and they pulled down the altar, and laid up the stones in the mountain of the house in a convenient place, until there should come a prophet to give an answer concerning them. And they took whole stones according to the law, and built a new altar after the fashion of the former; and they built the holy place, and the inner parts of the house; and they hallowed the courts. And they made the holy vessels new, and they brought the candlestick, and the altar of burnt offerings and of incense, and the table, into the temple. And they burned incense upon the altar, and they lighted the lamps that were upon the candlestick, and they gave light in the temple. And they set loaves upon the table, and spread out the veils, and finished all the works which they made.

And they rose up early in the morning, on the five and twentieth day of the ninth month, which is the month Chislev, in the hundred and forty and eighth year, and offered sacrifice according to the law upon the new altar of burnt offerings which they had made. At what time and on what day the Gentiles had profaned it, even on that day was it dedicated afresh, with songs and harps and lutes, and with cymbals. And all the people fell upon their faces, and worshipped, and gave praise unto heaven, which had given them good success. And they kept the dedication of the altar eight days, and offered burnt offerings with gladness, and sacrificed a sacrifice of deliverance and praise. And they decked the forefront of the temple with crowns of gold and small shields, and dedicated afresh the gates and the priests' chambers, and made doors for them. And there was exceeding great gladness among the people, and the reproach of the Gentiles was turned away. And Judas and his brethren and the whole congregation of Israel ordained, that the days of the dedication of the altar should be kept in their seasons from year to year by the space of eight days, from the five and twentieth day of the month Chislev, with gladness and joy. And at that season they builded up the mount Sion with high walls and strong towers round about, lest haply the Gentiles should come and tread them down, as they had done aforetime. And he set there a force to keep it, and they fortified Bethsura to keep it; that the people might have a stronghold over against Idumaea.

CHAPTER V

And it came to pass, when the Gentiles round about heard that the altar was built, and the sanctuary dedicated as aforetime, they were exceeding wroth. And they took counsel to destroy the race of Jacob that was in the midst of them, and they began to slay and destroy among the people. And Judas fought against the children of Esau in Idumaea at Akrabattine, because they besieged Israel: and he smote them with a great slaughter, and brought down their pride, and took their spoils. And he remembered the wickedness of the children of Baean, who were unto the people a snare and a stumblingblock, lying in wait for them in the ways. And they were shut up by him in the towers; and he encamped against them, and destroyed them utterly, and burned with fire the towers of the place, with all that were therein. And he passed over to the children of Ammon, and found a mighty band, and much people, with Timotheus for their leader. And he fought many battles with them, and they were discomfited before his face; and he smote them, and gat possession of Jazer, and the villages thereof, and returned again into Judea.

And the Gentiles that were in Gilead gathered themselves together against the Israelites that were on their borders, to destroy them. And they fled to the stronghold of Dathema, and sent letters unto Judas and his brethren, saying, The Gentiles that are round about us are gathered together against us to destroy us: and they are preparing to come and get possession of the stronghold whereunto we are fled for refuge, and Timotheus is the leader of their host. Now therefore come and deliver us from their hand, for many of us are fallen. And all our brethren that were in the land of Tubias have been put to death; and they have carried into captivity their wives and their children ;and their stuff; and they destroyed there about a thousand men. While the letters were yet reading, behold, there came other messengers from Galilee with their clothes rent, bringing a report after this wise, saying, That there were gathered together against them those of Ptolemais, and of Tyre, and of Sidon, and all Galilee of the Gentiles, to consume them.

Now when Judas and the people heard these words, there assembled together a great congregation, to consult what they should do for their brethren, that were in tribulation, and were assaulted of them. And Judas said unto Simon his brother, Choose thee out men, and go and deliver thy brethren that are in Galilee, but I and

Jonathon my brother will go into the land of Gilead. And he left Joseph the son of Zacharias, and Azarias, as leaders of the people, with the remnant of the host, in Judaea, for to keep it. And he gave commandment unto them, saying, Take ye the charge of this people, and fight no battle with the Gentiles until that we come again. And unto Simon were divided three thousand men to go into Galilee, but unto Judas eight thousand men to go into the land of Gilead.

And Simon went into Galilee, and fought many battles with the Gentiles, and the Gentiles were discomfited before him. And he pursued them unto the gate of Ptolemais; and there fell of the Gentiles about three thousand men, and he took their spoils. And they took to them those that were in Galilee, and in Arbatta, with their wives and their children, and all that they had, and brought them into Judaea with great gladness.

And Judas Maccabaeus and his brother Jonathan passed over Jordan, and went three days' journey in the wilderness; and they met with the Nabathaeans, and these met them in a peaceable manner, and told them all things that had befallen their brethren in the land of Gilead: and how that many of them were shut up in Bosora, and Bosor, and Alema, Casphor, Maked, and Carnaim; all these cities are strong and great: and how that they were shut up in the rest of the cities of the land of Gilead, and that to-morrow they have appointed to encamp against the strongholds, and to take them, and to destroy all these men in one day. And Judas and his army turned suddenly by the way of the wilderness unto Bosora; and he took the city, and slew all the males with the edge of the sword, and took; all their spoils, and burned the city with fire. And he removed from thence by night, and went till he came to the stronghold. And the morning came, and they lifted up their eyes, and, behold, much people which could not be numbered, bearing ladders and engines of war, to take the stronghold; and they were fighting against them. And Judas saw that the battle was begun, and that the cry of the city went up to heaven, with trumpets and a great sound, and he said unto the men of his host, Fight this day for your brethren. And he went forth behind them in three companies, and they sounded with their trumpets, and cried out in prayer. And the army of Timotheus perceived that it was Maccabaeus, and they fled from before him: and he smote them with a great slaughter; and there fell of them on that day about eight thousand men. And he turned aside to Mizpeh and fought against it, and took it, and slew all the males thereof, and took the spoils thereof; and burned it with fire. From thence he removed and took Casphor, Maked, Bosor, and the other cities of the land of Gilead.

Now after these things Timotheus gathered another army, and encamped over against Raphon beyond the brook. And Judas sent men to espy the army; and they brought him word, saying, All the Gentiles that be round about us are gathered together unto them, an exceeding great host. And they have hired Arabians to help them, and are encamping beyond the brook, ready to come against thee to battle. And Judas went to meet them. And Timotheus said unto the captains of his host, when Judas and his army drew nigh unto the brook of water, If he pass over first unto us, we shall not be able to withstand him; for he will mightily prevail against us: but if he be afraid, and encamp beyond the river, we will cross over unto him, and prevail against him. Now when Judas came nigh unto the brook of water, he caused the scribes of the people to remain by the brook, and gave commandment unto them, saying, Suffer no man to encamp, but let all come to the battle. And he crossed over the first against them, and all the people after him: and all the Gentiles were discomfited before his face, and cast away their arms, and fled unto the temple at

Carnaim. And they took the city, and burned the temple with fire, together with all that were therein. And Carnaim was subdued, neither could they stand any longer before the face of Judas.

And Judas gathered together all Israel, them that were in the land of Gilead, from the least unto the greatest, and their wives, and their children, and their stuff, an exceeding great army, that they might come into the land of Judah. And they came as far as Ephron, and this same city was great, and it was in the way as they should go, exceeding strong: they could not turn aside from it on the right hand or on the left, but must needs pass through the midst of it. And they of the city shut them out, and stopped up the gates with stones. And Judas sent unto them with words of peace, saying, We will pass through thy land to go into our own land, and none shall do you any hurt, we will only pass by on our feet. And they would not open unto him. And Judas commanded proclamation to be made in the army, that each man should encamp in the place where he was. And the men of the host encamped, and fought against the city all that day and all that night, and the city was delivered into his hands; and he destroyed all the males with the edge of the sword, and rased the city, and took the spoils thereof, and passed through the city over them that were slain. And they went over Jordan into the great plain over against Bethshan. And Judas gathered together those that lagged behind, and encouraged the people all the way through, until he came into the land of Judah. And they went up to mount Sion with gladness and joy, and offered whole burnt offerings, because not so much as one of them was slain until they returned in peace.

And in the days when Judas and Jonathan were in the land of Gilead, and Simon his brother in Galilee before Ptolemais, Joseph the son of Zacharias, and Azarias, rulers of the host, heard of their exploits and of the war, what things they had done; and they said, Let us also get us a name, and let us go fight against the Gentiles that are round about us. And they gave charge unto the men of the host that was with them, and went toward Jamnia. And Gorgias and his men came out of the city to meet them in battle. And Joseph and Azarias were put to flight, and were pursued unto the borders of Judaea; and there fell on that day of the people of Israel about two thousand men. And there was a great overthrow among the people, because they hearkened not unto Judas and his brethren, thinking to do some exploit. But they were not of the seed of those men, by whose hand deliverance was given unto Israel.

And the man Judas and his brethren were glorified exceedingly in the sight of all Israel, and of all the Gentiles, wheresoever their name was heard of; and men gathered together unto them, acclaiming them.

And Judas and his brethren went forth, and fought against the children of Esau in the land toward the south; and he smote Hebron and the villages thereof, and pulled down the strongholds thereof, and burned the towers thereof round about. And he removed to go into the land of the Philistines, and he went through Samaria. In that day certain priests, desiring to do exploits there, were slain in battle, when as he went out to battle unadvisedly. And Judas turned aside to Azotus, to the land of the Philistines, and pulled down their altars, and burned the carved images of their gods with fire, and took the spoil of their cities, and returned into the land of Judah.

CHAPTER VI

And king Antiochus was journeying through the upper countries; and he heard say, that in Elymais in Persia there was a city renowned for riches, for silver and gold; and that the temple which was in it was rich exceedingly, and that therein were golden shields, and breastplates, and arms, which Alexander, son of Philip, the Macedonian king, who reigned first among the Greeks, left behind there. And he came and sought to take the city, and to pillage it; and he was not able, because the thing was known to them of the city, and they rose up against him to battle: and he fled, and removed thence with great heaviness, to return unto Babylon.

And there came one bringing him tidings into Persia, that the armies, which went against the land of Judah, had been put to flight; and that Lysias went first with a strong host, and was put to shame before them; and that they had waxed strong by reason of arms and power, and with store of spoils, which they took from the armies that they had cut off; and that they had pulled down the abomination which he had built upon the altar that was in Jerusalem; and that they had compassed about the sanctuary with high walls, as before, and Bethsura, his city. And it came to pass, when the king heard these words, he was astonished and moved exceedingly: and he laid him down upon his bed, and fell sick for grief, because it had not befallen him as he looked for. And he was there many days, because great grief was renewed upon him, and he made account that he should die. And he called for all his Friends, and said unto them, Sleep departeth from mine eyes, and my heart faileth for care. And I said in my heart, Unto what tribulation am I come, and how great a flood is it, wherein I now am ! for I was gracious and beloved in my power. But now I remember the evils which I did at Jerusalem, and that I took all the vessels of silver and gold that were therein, and sent forth to destroy the inhabitants of Judah without a cause. I perceive that on this account these evils are come upon me, and, behold, I perish through great grief in a strange land. And he called for Philip, one of his

Friends, and set him over all his kingdom, and gave him his diadem, and his robe, and his signet-ring, to the end he should bring Antiochus his son, and nourish him up that he might be king. And king Antiochus died there in the hundred and forty and ninth year. And Lysias knew that the king was dead, and he set up Antiochus his son to reign, whom he had nourished up being young, and he called his name Eupator.

And they that were in the citadel shut up Israel round about the sanctuary, and sought always their hurt, and the strengthening of the Gentiles. And Judas thought to destroy them, and called all the people together to besiege them. And they were gathered together, and besieged them in the hundred and fiftieth year, and he made mounds to shoot from, and engines of war. And there came forth some of them that were shut up, and there were joined unto them certain ungodly men of Israel. And they went unto the king, and said, How long wilt thou not execute judgement, and avenge our brethren? We were willing to serve thy father, and to walk after his words, and to follow his commandments; and for this cause the children of our people besieged the citadel, and were alienated from us; but as many of us as they could light on they slew, and spoiled our inheritances. And not against us only did they stretch out their hand, but also against all their borders. And, behold, they are encamped this day against the citadel at Jerusalem, to take it: and the sanctuary and Bethsura have they fortified. And if ye are not beforehand with them quickly, they will do greater things than these, and thou shalt not be able to control them.

And when the king heard this, he was angry, and gathered together all his Friends, even the rulers of his host, and them that were over the horse. And there came unto him from other kingdoms, and from isles of the sea, bands of hired soldiers. And the number of his forces was a hundred thousand footmen, and twenty thousand horsemen, and two and thirty elephants trained for war. And they went through Idumaea, and encamped against Bethsura, and fought against it many days, and made engines of war; and they of Bethsura came out, and burn ed them with fire, and fought valiantly. And Judas removed from the citadel, and encamped at Bethzacharias, over against the king's camp. And the king rose early in the morning, and removed his army at full speed along the road to Bethzacharias, and his forces made them ready to battle, and sounded with the trumpets. And they shewed the elephants the blood of grapes and mulberries, that they might prepare them for the battle. And they divided the beasts among the phalanxes, and they set by each elephant a thousand men armed with coats of mail, and helmets of brass on their heads; and for each beast were appointed five hundred chosen horsemen. These were ready beforehand, wheresoever the beast was; and whithersoever the beast went, they went with him; they departed not from him. And towers of wood were upon them, strong and covered, one upon each beast, girt fast upon him with cunning contrivances; and upon each beast were two and thirty valiant men that fought upon them, beside his Indian (and the residue of the horsemen he set on this side and that side at the two parts of the army), striking terror into the enemy, and protected by the phalanxes. Now when the sun shone upon the shields of gold and brass, the mountains shone therewith, and blazed like torches of fire. And a part of the king's army was spread upon the high mountains, and some on the low ground, and they went on firmly and in order. And all that heard the noisc of their multitude, and the marching of the multitude, and the rattling of the arms, did quake: for the army was exceeding great and strong. And Judas and his army drew near for battle, and there fell of the king's army six hundred men. And

Eleazar, who was called Avaran, saw one of the beasts armed with royal breastplates, and he was higher than all the beasts, and the king seemed to be upon him; and he gave himself to deliver his people, and to get him an everlasting name; and he ran upon him courageously into the midst of the phalanx, and slew on the right hand and on the left, and they parted asunder from him on this side and on that. And he crept under the elephant, and thrust him from beneath, and slew him; and the elephant fell to the earth upon him, and he died there. And they saw the strength of the kingdom, and the fierce onset of the hosts, and turned away from them.

But they of the king's army went up to Jerusalem to meet them, and the king encamped toward Judea, and toward mount Sion. And he made peace with them of Bethsura; and he came out of the city, because they had no food there to endure the siege, because it was a sabbath to the land. And the king took Bethsura, and appointed a garrison there to keep it. And he encamped against the sanctuary many days; and set there mounds to shoot from, and engines of war, and instruments for casting fire and stones, and pieces to cast darts, and slings. And they also made engines against their engines, and fought for many days. But there were no victuals in the sanctuary, because it was the seventh year, and they that fled for safety into Judea from among the Gentiles had eaten up the residue of the store; and there were but a few left in the sanctuary, because the famine prevailed against them, and they were scattered, each man to his own place.

And Lysias heard say, that Philip, whom Antiochus the king, whiles he was yet alive, appointed to nourish up his son Antiochus, that he might be king, was returned from Persia and Media, and with him the forces that went with the king, and that he was seeking to take unto him the government. And he made haste, and gave consent to depart; and he said to the king and the leaders of the host and to the men, We decay daily, and our food is scant, and the place where we encamp is strong, and the affairs of the kingdom lie upon us: now therefore let us give the right hand to these men, and make peace with them and with all their nation, and covenant with them, that they shall walk after their own laws, as aforetime: for because of their laws which we abolished they were angered, and did all these things. And the saying pleased the king and the princes, and he sent unto them to make peace; and they accepted thereof. And the king and the princes sware unto them: thereupon they came forth from the stronghold. And the king entered into mount Sion; and he saw the strength of the place, and set at nought the oath which he had sworn, and gave commandment to pull down the wall round about. And he removed in haste, and returned unto Antioch, and found Philip master of the city; and he fought against him, and took the city by force.

CHAPTER VII

In the hundred and one and fiftieth year Demetrius the son of Seleucus came forth from Rome, and went up with a few men unto a city by the sea, and reigned there. And it came to pass, when he would go into the house of the kingdom of his fathers, that the army laid hands on Antiochus and Lysias, to bring them unto him. And the thing was known to him, and he said, Shew me not their faces. And the army slew them. And Demetrius sat upon the throne of his kingdom. And there came unto him all the lawless and ungodly men of Israel ; and

Alcimus was their leader, desiring to be high priest; and they accused the people to the king, saying, Judas and his brethren have destroyed all thy friends, and have scattered us from our own land. Now therefore send a man whom thou trustest, and let him go and see all the havock which he hath made of us, and of the king's country, and how he hath punished them and all that helped them. And the king chose Bacchides, one of the king's Friends, who was ruler in the country beyond the river, and was a great man in the kingdom, and faithful to the king. And he sent him, and that ungodly Alcimus, and made sure to him the high priesthood, and he commanded him to take vengeance upon the children of Israel.

And they removed, and came with a great host into the land of Judah, and he sent messengers to Jadas and his brethren with words of peace deceitfully. And they gave no heed to their words; for they saw that they were come with a great host. And there were gathered together unto Alcimus and Bacchides a company of scribes, to seek for justice. And the Hasideans were the first among the children of Israel that sought peace of them; for they said, One that is a priest of the seed of Aaron is come with the forces, and he will do us no wrong. And he spake with them words of peace, and sware unto them, saying, We will seek the hurt neither of you nor your friends. And they gave him credence: and he laid hands on threescore men of them, and slew them in one day, according to the word which the psalmist wrote, The flesh of thy saints did they cast out, and their blood did they shed round about Jerusalem; and there was no man to bury them.

And the fear and the dread of them fell upon all the people, for they said, There is neither truth nor judgement in them; for they have broken the covenant and the oath which they sware. And Bacchides removed from Jerusalem, and encamped in Bezeth; and he sent and took many of the deserters that were with him, and certain of the people; and he slew them, and cast them into the great pit. And he made sure the country to Alcimus, and left with him a force to aid him; and Bacchides went away unto the king.

And Alcimus strove for his high priesthood. And there were gathered unto him all they that troubled their people, and they got the mastery of the land of Judah, and did great hurt in Israel. And Judas saw all the mischief that Alcimus and his company had done among the children of Israel, even above the Gentiles, and he went out into all the coasts of Judea round about, and took vengeance on the men that had deserted from him, and they were restrained from going forth into the country. But when Alcimus saw that Judas and his company waxed strong, and knew that he was not able to withstand them, he returned to the king, and brought evil accusations against them.

And the king sent Nicanor, one of his honourable princes a man that hated Israel and was their enemy and commanded him to destroy the people. And Nicanor came to Jerusalem with a great host; and he sent unto Judas and his brethren deceitfully with words of peace, saying, Let there be no battle between me and you; I will come with a few men, that I may see your faces in peace. And he came to Judas, and they saluted one another peaceably. And the enemies were ready to take away Judas by violence. And the thing was known to Judas, to wit, that he came unto him with deceit, and he was sore afraid of him, and would see his face no more. And Nicanor knew that his counsel was discovered; and he went out to meet Judas in battle beside Capharsalama; and there fell of Nicanor's side about five hundred men, and they fled into the city of David.

And after these things Nicanor went up to mount Sion: and there came some of the priests out of the sanctuary, and some of the elders of the people, to salute him peaceably, and to shew him the whole burnt sacrifice that was being offered for the king. And he mocked them, and laughed at them, and entreated them shamefully, and spake haughtily, and sware in a rage, saying, Unless Judas and his army be now delivered into my hands, it shall be that, if I come again in peace, I will burn up this house: and he went out in a great rage. And the priest entered in, and stood before the alter and the temple; and they wept, and said, Thou didst choose this house to be called by thy name, to be a house of prayer and supplication for thy people: take vengeance on this man and his army, and let them fall by the sword: remember their blasphemies, and suffer them not to live any longer.

And Nicanor went forth from Jerusalem, and encamped in Bethhoron, and there met him the host of Syria. And Judas encamped in Adasa with three thousand men: and Judas prayed and said, When they that came from the king blasphemed, thine angel went out, and smote among them a hundred and four-score and five thousand. Even so discomfit thou this army before us to-day, and let all the rest know that he hath spoken wickedly against thy sanctuary, and judge thou him according to his wickedness. And on the thirteenth day of the month Adar the armies joined battle: and Nicanor's army was discomfited, and he himself was the first to fall in the battle. Now when his army saw that Nicanor was fallen, they cast away their arms, and fled. And they pursued after them a day's journey from Adasa until thou comest to Gazara, and they sounded an alarm after them with the solemn trumpets. And they came forth out of all the villages of Judea round about, and closed them in; and these turned them back on those, and they all fell by the sword, and there was not one of them left. And they took spoils, and the booty, and they smote off Nicanor's head, and his right hand, which he stretched out so haughtily, and brought them, and hanged them up beside Jerusalem. And the people was exceeding glad, and they kept that day as a day of great gladness. And they ordained to keep this day year by year, to wit, the thirteenth day of Adar. And the land of Judah had rest a little while.

CHAPTER VIII

AND Judas heard of the fame of the Romans, that they are valiant men, and have pleasure in all that join themselves unto them, and make amity with all such as come unto them, and that they are valiant men. And they told him of their wars and exploits which they do among the Gauls, and how that they conquered them, and brought them under tribute; and what things they did in the land of Spain, that they might become masters of the mines of silver and gold which were there; and how that by their policy and persistence they conquered all the place (and the place was exceeding far from them), and the kings that came against them from the uttermost part of the earth, until they had discomfited them and smitten them very sore; and how the rest give them tribute year by year; and Philip, and Perseus, king of Chittim, and them that lifted up themselves against them, did they discomfit in battle, and conquered them: Antiochus also, the great king of Asia, who came against them to battle, having a hundred and twenty elephants, with horse, and chariots, and an exceeding great host, and he was discomfited by them, and they took him alive, and appointed that both he and such as reigned after him should give them a great tribute, and should give hostages, and a parcel of land, to wit, the country of India, and Media, and Lydia, and of the goodliest of their countries; and they took them from him, and gave them to king Eumenes: and how they of Greece took counsel to come and destroy them; and the thing was known to them, and they sent against them a captain, and fought against them, and many of them fell down wounded to death, and they made captive their wives and their children, and spoiled them, and conquered their land, and pulled down their strongholds, and spoiled them, and brought them into bondage unto this day: and the residue of the kingdoms and of the isles, as many as rose up against them at any time, they destroyed and made them to be their servants; but with their friends and such as relied upon them they kept amity; and they conquered the kingdoms that were nigh and those that were far off, and all that heard of their fame were afraid of them: moreover, whomsoever they will to succour and to make kings, these do they make kings; and whomsoever they will, do they depose; and they are exalted exceedingly: and for all this none of them did ever put on a diadem, neither did they clothe themselves with purple, to be magnified thereby: and how they had made for themselves a senate house, and day by day three hundred and twenty men sat in council, consulting alway for the people, to the end they might be well ordered: and how they commit their government to one man year by year, that he should rule over them, and be lord over all their country, and all are obedient to that one, and there is neither envy nor emulation among them.

And Judas chose Eupolemus the son of John, the son of Accos, and Jason the son of Eleazar, and sent them to Rome, to make a league of amity and confederacy with them, and that they should take the yoke from them; for they saw that the kingdom of the Greeks did keep Israel in bondage. And they went to Rome (and the way was exceeding long), and they entered into the senate house, and answered and said, Judas, who is also called Maccabeaus, and his brethren, and the people of the Jews, have sent us unto you, to make a confederacy and peace with you, and that we might be registered your confederates and friends.

And the thing was well-pleasing in their sight. And this is the copy of the writing which they wrote back again on tables of brass, and sent to Jerusalem, that it might be with them there for a memorial of peace and confederacy:

Good success be to the Romans, and to the nation of the Jews, by sea and land for ever: the sword also and the enemy be far from them. But if war arise for Rome first, or any of their confederates in all their dominion, the nation of the Jews shall help them as confederates, as the occasion shall prescribe to them, with all their heart: and unto them that make war upon them they shall not give, neither supply, food, arms, money, or ships, as it hath seemed good unto Rome, and they shall keep their ordinances without taking anything therefore. In the same manner, moreover, if war come first upon the nation of the Jews, the Romans shall help them as confederates with all their soul, as the occasion shall prescribe to them: and so to them that are confederates with their foes there shall not be given food, arms, money or ships, as it hath seemed good unto Rome; and they shall keep these ordinances and that without deceit. According to these words have the Romans made a covenant thus with the people of the Jews. But if hereafter the one party and the other shall take counsel to add or diminish anything, they shall do it at their pleasure, and whatsoever they shall add or take away shall be established. And as touching the evils which king Demetrius doeth unto them, we have written to him, saying, Wherefore hast thou made thy yoke heavy upon our friends and confederates the Jews? If therefore they plead any more against thee, we will do them justice, and fight with thee by sea and by land.

CHAPTER IX

AND Demetrius heard that Nicanor was fallen with his forces in battle, and he sent Bacchides and Alcimus again into the land of Judah a second time, and the right wing of his army with them: and they went by the way that leadeth to Gilgal, and encamped against Mesaloth, which is in Arbela, and gat possession of it, and destroyed much people. And the first month of the hundred and fifty and second year they encamped against Jerusalem: and they removed, and went to Berea, with twenty thousand footmen and two thousand horse. And Judas was encamped at Elasa, and three thousand chosen men with him: and they saw the multitude of the forces, that they were many, and they feared exceedingly: and many slipped away out of the army; there were not left of them more than eight hundred men. And Judas saw that his army slipped away, and that the battle pressed upon him, and he was sore troubled in heart, for that he had no time to gather them together, and he waxed faint. And he said to them that were left, Let us arise and go up against our adversaries, if peradventure we may be able to fight with them. And they would have dissuaded him, saying, We shall in no wise be able: but let us rather save our lives now: let us return again, we and our brethren, and fight against them: but we are few. And Judas said, Let it not be so that I should do this thing, to flee from them: and if our time is come, let us die manfully for our brethren's sake and not leave a cause of reproach against our glory. And the host removed from the camp, and stood to encounter them, and the horse was parted into two companies, and the slingers and the archers went before the host, and all the mighty men that fought in the front of the battle. But Bacchides was in the right wing; and the phalanx drew near on the two parts, and they blew with their trumpets. And the men of Judas' side even they sounded with their trumpets, and the earth shook with the shout of the armies, and the battle was joined, and continued from morning until evening. And Judas saw that Bacchides and the strength of his army were on the right side, and there went with him all that were brave in heart, and the right wing was discomfited by them, and he pursued after them unto the mount Azotus. And they that were on the left wing saw that the right wing was discomfited, and they turned and followed upon the footsteps of Judas and of those that were with him: and the battle waxed sore, and many on both parts fell wounded to death. And Judas fell, and the rest fled. And Jonathan and Simon took Judas their brother, and buried him in the sepulcher of his fathers at Modin. And they bewailed him, and all Israel made great lamentation for him, and mourned many days, and said, How is the mighty fallen, the saviour of Israell And the rest of the acts of Judas, and his wars, and the valiant deeds which he did, and his greatness, they are not written; for they were exceeding many.

And it came to pass after the death of Judas, that the lawless put forth their heads in all the coasts, of Israel, and all they that wrought iniquity rose up (in those days was there an exceeding great famine), and the country went over with them. And Bacchides chose out the ungodly men, 'and made them lords of the country. And they sought,out and searched for the friends of Judas, and brought them unto Bacchides, and he took vengeance on them, and used them despitefully. And there was great tribulation in Israel, such as was not since the time that no prophet appeared unto them. And all the friends of Judas were gathered together, and they said unto Jonathan, Since thy brother Judas hath died, we have no man like him to go forth against our enemies and Bacchides, and among them of our nation that hate us.

Now therefore we have chosen thee this day to be our prince and leader in his stead, that thou mayest fight our battles. And Jonathan took the governance upon him at that time, and rose up in the stead of his brother Judas.

And Bacchides knew it, and he sought to slay him. And Jonathan, and Simon his brother, and all that were with him, knew it; and they fled into the wilderness of Tekoah, and encamped by the water of the pool Asphar. And Bacchides knew it on the sabbath day, and came, he and all his army, over Jordan. And Jonathan sent his brother, a leader of the multitude, and besought his friends the Nabathaeans, that they might leave with them their baggage, which was much. And the children of Jambri came out of Medaba, and took John, and all that he had, and went their way with it.

But after these things they brought word to Jonathan and Simon his brother, that the children of Jambri were making a great marriage, and were bringing the bride from Nadabath with a great train, a daughter of one of the great nobles of Canaan. And they remembered John their brother, and went up, and hid themselves under the covert of the mountain: and they lifted up their eyes, and saw, and, behold, a great ado and much baggage: and the bridegroom came forth, and his friends and his brethren, to meet them with timbrels, and minstrels, and many weapons. And they rose up against them from their ambush, and slew them, and many fell wounded to death, and the remnant fled into the mountain, and they took all their spoils. And the marriage was turned into mourning, and the voice of their minstrels into lamentation. And they avenged fully the blood of their brother, and turned back to the marsh of Jordan.

And Bacchides heard it, and he came on the sabbath day unto the banks of Jordan with a great host. And Jonathan said to his company, Let us stand up now and fight for our lives, for it is not with us today, as yesterday and the day before. For, behold, the battle is and before us, and behind us; moreover the water of the Jordan is on this side and on that side, and marsh and wood; and there is no place to turn aside. Now therefore cry unto heaven, that ye may be delivered out of the hand of your enemies. And the battle was joined, and Jonathan stretched forth his hand to smite Bacchides, and he turned away back from him. And Jonathan and they that were with him leapt into the Jordan, and swam over to the other side: and they did not pass over Jordan against them. And there fell of Bacchides' company that day about a thousand men; and he returned to Jerusalem. And they builded strong cities in Judea, the stronghold that was in Jericho, and Emmaus, and Bethhoron, and Bethel, and Timnath, Pharathon, and Tephon, with high walls and gates and bars. And in them he set a garrison, to vex Israel. And he fortified the city Bethsura, and Gazara, and the citadel, and put forces in them, and store of victuals. And he took the sons of the chief men of the country for hostages, and put them in ward in the citadel at Jerusalem

And in the hundred and fifty and third year, in the second month, Alcimus commanded to pull down the wall of the inner court of the sanctuary; he pulled down also the works of the prophets; and he began to pull down. At that time was Alcimus stricken, and his works were hindered; and his mouth was stopped, and he was taken with a palsy, and he could no more speak anything and give order concerning his house, and Alcimus died at that time with great torment. And Bacchides saw that Alcimus was dead, and he returned to the king: and the land of Judah had rest two years.

And all the lawless men took counsel, saying, Behold, Jonathan and they of his part are dwelling at ease, and in security: now therefore we will bring Bacchides, and he shall lay hands on them all in one night. And they went and consulted with him. And he removed, and came with a great host, and sent letters privily to all his confederates that were in Judea, that they should lay hands on Jonathan and those that were with him: and they could not, because their counsel was known unto them. And they that were of Jonathan's part laid hands on about fifty of the men of the country, that were authors of the wickedness, and he slew them. And Jonathan, and Simon, and they that were with him, gat them away to Bethbasi, which is in the wilderness, and he built up that which had been pulled down thereof, and they made it strong. And Bacchides knew it, and he gathered together all his multitude, and sent word to them that were of Judea. And he went and encamped against Bethbasi, and fought against it many days, and made engines of war. And Jonathan left his brother Simon in the city, and went forth into the country, and he went with a few men. And he smoke Odomera and his brethren, and the children of Phasiron in their tent. And they began to smite them, and to go up with their forces. And Simon and they that were with him went out of the city, and set on fire the engines of war, and fought against Bacchides, and he was discomfited by them, and they afflicted him sore; for his counsel was in vain, and his inroad. And they were very wroth with the lawless men that gave him counsel to come into the country, and they slew many of them. And he took counsel to depart into his own land. And Jonathan had knowledge thereof, and sent ambassadors unto him, to the end that they should make peace with him, and that he should restore unto them the captives. And he accepted the thing, and did according to his words, and sware unto him that he would not seek his hurt all the days of his life. And he restored unto him the captives which he had taken aforetime out of the land of Judah, and he returned and departed into his own land, and came not any more into their borders. And the sword ceased from Israel.

And Jonathan dwelt at Michmash; and Jonathan began to judge the people; and he destroyed the ungodly out of Israel.

CHAPTER X

AND in the hundred and sixtieth year Alexander Epiphanies, the son of Antiochus, went up and took possession of Ptolemais; and they received him, and he reigned there. And king Demetrius heard thereof, and he gathered together exceeding great forces, and went forth to meet him in battle.

And Demetrius sent letters unto Jonathan with words of peace, so as to magnify him. For he said, Let us be beforehand to make peace with them, ere he make peace with Alexander against us: for he will remember all the evils that we have done against him, and unto his brethren and unto his nation. And he gave him authority to gather together forces, and to provide arms, and that he should be his confederate: and he commanded that they should deliver up to him the hostages that were in the citadel.

And Jonathan came to Jerusalem, and read the letters in the audience of all the people, and of them that were in the citadel: and they were sore afraid, when they heard that the king had given him authority to gather together a host. And they of the citadel delivered up the hostages unto Jonathan, and he restored them unto their parents. And Jonathan dwelt in Jerusalem, and began to build and renew the city. And he commanded them that did the work to build the walls and the mount Sion round about with square stones for defence; and they did so. And the strangers, that were in the strongholds which Bacchides had built, fled away; and each man left his place, and departed into his own land. Only at Bethsura were there left certain of those that had forsaken the law and the commandments; for it was a place of refuge unto them.

And king Alexander heard all the promises which Demetrius had sent unto Jonathan; and they told him of the battles and the valiant deeds which he and his brethren had done, and of the toils which they had endured; and he said, Shall we find such another man? and now we will make him our Friend and confederate. And he wrote letters, and sent them unto him, according to these words, saying,

King Alexander to his brother Jonathan, greeting: We have heard of thee, that thou art a mightily man of valour, and meet to be our Friend. And now we have appointed thee this day to be high priest of thy nation, and to be called the king's Friend (and he sent unto him a purple robe and a crown of gold), and to take our part, and to keep friendship with us.

And Jonathan put on the holy garments in the seventh month of the hundred and sixtieth year, at the feast of tabernacles, and he gathered together forces and provided arms in abundance.

And Demetrius heard these things, and he was grieved, and said, What is this that we have done, that Alexander hath been beforehand with us in establishing friendship with the Jews, to strengthen himself? I also will write unto them words of encouragement and of honour and of gifts, that they may be with me to aid me. And he sent unto them according to these words: King Demetrius unto the nation of the Jews, greetings: Forasmuch as ye have kept your covenants with us, and continued in our friendship, and have not joined yourselves to our enemies, we have heard hereof, and are glad. And now continue ye still to keep faith with us, and we will recompense unto you good things in return for your dealings with us, and will grant you many immunities, and give you gifts. And now do I free you, and release all the Jews, from the tributes, and from the customs of salt, and from the crowns. And instead of the third part of the seed, and instead of the half of the fruit of the trees, which falleth to me to receive, I release it from this day and henceforth, so that I will not take it from the land of Judah, and from the three governments which are added thereunto from the country of Samaria and Galilee, from this day forth and for all time. And let Jerusalem be holy and free, and her borders; the tenths and the tolls also. I yield up also my authority over the citadel which is at Jerusalem, and give it to the high priest, that he may appoint in it such men as he shall choose to keep it. And every soul of the Jews, that hath been carried captive from the land of Judah into any part of my kingdom, I set at liberty without price; and let all remit the tributes of their cattle also. And all the feasts, and the sabbaths, and new moons, and appointed days, and three days before a feast, and three days after a feast, let them all be days of immunity and release for all the Jews that are in my kingdom. And no man shall have authority to exact from any of them, or to trouble them concerning any matter. And let there be enrolled among the king's forces about thirty thousand men of the Jews, and pay shall be given unto them, as belongeth to all the king's forces. And of them some shall be placed in the king's great strongholds, and some of them shall be placed over the affairs of the kingdom, which are of trust: and let those that are over them, and their rulers, be of themselves, and let them walk after their own laws, even as the king hath commanded in the land of Judah. And the three governments that have been added to Judaea from the country of Samaria, let them be added to Judaea, that they may be reckoned to be under one, that they may not obey other authority than the high priest's. As for Ptolemais, and the land pertaining thereto, I have given it as a gift to the sanctuary that is at Jerusalem, for the expenses that befit the sanctuary And I give every year fifteen thousand shekels of silver from the king's revenues from the places that are convenient. And all the overplus, which they that manage the king's affairs paid not in as in the first years, they shall give from henceforth toward the works of the house. And beside this, the five thousand shekels of silver, which they received from the uses of the sanctuary from the revenue year by year, this also is released, because it appertaineth to the priests that minister. And whosoever shall flee unto the temple that is at Jerusalem, and be found within all the borders thereof, whether one owe moneys to the king, or any other matter, let them go free, and all that they have in my kingdom. And for the building and renewing of the works of the sanctuary the expense shall be given also out of the king's revenue. And for the building of the walls of Jerusalem, and the fortifying thereof round about, shall the expense be given also out of the king's revenue, and for the building of the walls in Judaea

Now when Jonathan and the people heard these words, they gave no credence unto them, nor received them, because they remembered the great evil which he had done in Israel, and that he had afflicted them very sore. And they were well pleased with Alexander, because he was the first that spake words of peace unto them, and they were confederate with him always. And king Alexander gathered together great forces, and encamped over against Demetrius. And the two kings joined battle, and the army of Alexander fled; and Demetrius followed after him, and prevailed against them. And he strengthened the battle exceedingly until the sun went down: and Demetrius fell that day.

And Alexander sent ambassadors to Ptolemy king of Egypt according to these words, saying, Forasmuch as I am returned to my kingdom, and am set on the throne of my fathers, and have gotten the dominion, and have overthrown Demetrius, and have gotten our country; yea, I joined battle with him, and he and his army were discomfited by us, and we sat upon the throne of his kingdom: now also let us establish amity one with the other, and give me now thy daughter to wife: and I will make affinity with thee, and will give both thee and her gifts worthy of thee. And Ptolemy the king answered, saying, Happy is the day wherein thou didst return into the land of thy fathers, and didst sit on the throne of their kingdom. And now will I do to thee, as thou hast written: but meet me at Ptolemais, that we may see one another; and I will make affinity with thee, even as thou hast said. And Ptolemy went out of Egypt, himself and Cleopatra his daughter, and came unto Ptolemais in the hundred and threescore and second year: and king Alexander met him, and he bestowed on him his daughter Cleopatra, and celebrated her marriage at Ptolemais with great pomp, as the manner of kings is.

And king Alexander wrote unto Jonathan, that he should come to meet him. And he went with pomp to Ptolemais, and met the two kings, and gave them and their Friends silver and gold, and many gifts, and found favour in their sight. And there were gathered together against him certain pestilent fellows out of Israel, men that were transgressors of the law, to complain against him: and the king gave no heed to them. And the king commanded, and they took off Jonathan's garments, and clothed him in purple: and thus they did And the king made him sit with him, and said unto his princes, Go forth with him into the midst of the city, and make proclamation, that no man complain against him of any matter, and let no man trouble him for any manner of cause. And it came to pass, when they that complained against him saw his glory according as the herald made proclamation, and saw him clothed in purple, they all fled away. And the king gave him honour, and wrote him among his Chief Friends, and made him a captain, and governor of a province. And Jonathan returned to Jerusalem with peace and gladness.

And in the hundred and threescore and fifth year came Demetrius, son of Demetrius, out of Crete into the land of his fathers: and king Alexander heard thereof, and he was grieved exceedingly, and returned unto Antioch. And Demetrius appointed Apollonius, who was over Coelesyria, and he gathered together a great host, and encamped in Jamnia, and sent unto Jonathan the high priest, saying,

Thou alone liftest up thyself against us, but I am had in derision and in reproach because of thee. And why dost thou vaunt thy power against us in the mountains? Now therefore, if thou trustest in thy forces, come down to us into the plain, and there let us try the matter together; for with me is the power of the cities. Ask and learn who I am, and the rest that help us; and they say, Your foot cannot stand before our face; for thy fathers have been twice put to flight in their own land. And now thou shalt not be able to abide the horse and such a host as this in the plain, where is neither stone nor flint, nor place to flee unto.

Now when Jonathan heard the words of Apollonius, he was moved in his mind, and he chose out ten thousand men, and went forth from Jerusalem, and Simon his brother met him for to help him. And he encamped against Joppa: and they of the city shut him out, because Apollonius had a garrison in Joppa: and they fought against it. And they of the city were afraid, and opened unto him: and Jonathan became master of Joppa. And Apollonius heard, and he gathered an army of three thousand horse, and a great host, and went to Azotus as though he were on a journey, and therewithal drew onward into the plain, because he had a multitude of horse, and trusted therein. And he pursued after him to Azotus, and the armies joined battle. And Apollonius had left a thousand horse behind them privity. And Jonathan knew that there was an ambushment behind him. And they compassed round his army, and cast their darts at the people, from morning until evening: but the people stood still, as Jonathan commanded them: and their horses were wearied. And Simon drew forth his host, and joined battle with the phalanx (for the horsemen were spent), and they were discomfited by him, and fled And the horsemen were scattered in the plain, and they fled to Azotus, and entered into Beth-dagon, their idol's temple, to save themselves. And Jonathan burned Azotus, and the cities round about it, and took their spoils; and the temple of Dagon, and them that fled into it, he burned with fire. And they that had fallen by the sword, with them that were burned, were about eight thousand men. And from thence Jonathan removed, and encamped against Ascalon, and they of the city came forth to meet him with great pomp. And Jonathan, with them that were on his side, returned unto Jerusalem, having many spoils. And it came to pass, when king Alexander heard these things, he honoured Jonathan yet more; and he sent unto him a buckle of gold, as the use is to give to such as are of the kindred of the kings: and he gave him Ekron and all the coasts thereof for a possession.

CHAPTER XI

AND the king of Egypt gathered together great forces, as the sand which is by the sea shore, and many ships, and sought to make himself master of Alexander's kingdom by deceit, and to add it to his own kingdom. And he went forth into Syria with words of peace, and they of the cities opened unto him, and met him; for king Alexander's commandment was that they should meet him, because he was his father in law.

Now as he entered into the cities of Ptolemais, he set his forces for a garrison in each city. But when he came near to Azotus, they shewed him the temple of Dagon burned with fire, and Azotus and the suburbs thereof pulled down, and the bodies cast abroad, and them that had been burned, whom he burned in the war for they had made heaps of them in his way. And they told the king what things Jonathan had done, that they might cast blame on him: and the king held his peace. And Jonathan met the king with pomp at Joppa, and they saluted one another, and they slept there: And Jonathan went with the king as far as the river that is called Eleutherus, and returned to Jerusalem. But king Ptolemy became master of the cities upon the sea coast, unto Seleucia which is by the sea, and he devised evil devices concerning Alexander. And he sent ambassadors unto king Demetrius, saying, Come, let us make a covenant with one another, and I will give thee my daughter whom Alexander hath, and thou shalt reign over they father's kingdom: for I have repented that I gave my daughter unto him, for he sought to slay me. And he cast blame on him, because he coveted his kingdom. And taking his daughter from him, he gave her to Demetrius, and was estranged from Alexander, and their enmity was openly seen. And Ptolemy entered into Antioch, and put on himself the diadem of Asia, and he put two diadems upon his head, the diadem of Egypt and that of Asia. But king Alexander was in Cilicia at that season, because they of those parts were in revolt. And Alexander heard of it, and he came against him in war: and Ptolemy led forth his host, and met him with a strong force, and put him to flight. And Alexander fled into Arabia, that he might be sheltered there; but king Ptolemy was exalted. And Zabdiel the Arabian took off Alexander's head, and sent it to Ptolemy. And king Ptolemy died the third day after, and they that were in his strangleholds were slain by them that were in the strongholds. And Demetrius reigned in the hundred and threescore and seventh year.

In those days Jonathan gathered together them of Judea, to take the citadel that was at Jerusalem: and he made many engines of war against it. And certain that hated their own nation, men that transgressed the law, went unto the king, and reported to him that Jonathan was besieging the citadel. And he heard and was angered; but when he heard it, he set forth immediately, and came to Ptolemais, and wrote unto Jonathan, that he should not besiege it, and that he should meet him and speak with him at Ptolemais with all speed. But when Jonathan heard this, he commanded to besiege it still: and he chose certain of the elders of Israel and of the priests, and put himself in peril, and taking silver and gold and raiment and divers presents besides, went to Ptolemais unto the king. And he found favour in his sight. And certain lawless men of them that were of the nation made complaints against him, and the king did unto him even as his predecessor had done unto him, and exalted him in the sight of all his Friends, and confirmed to him the high priesthood, and all the other honour that he had before, and gave him pre-eminence among his Chief Friends. And Jonathan requested of the king, that he would make Judea free from tribute, and the three provinces, and the country of Samaria; and promised him three hundred talents. And the king consented, and wrote letters unto Jonathan concerning all these things after this manner:

King Demetrius unto his brother Jonathan, and unto the nation of the Jews, greeting: The copy of the letter which we wrote unto Lasthenes our kinsman concerning you, we have written also unto you, that ye may see it. King Demetrius unto Lasthenes his father, greeting: We have determined to do good to the nation of the Jews, who are our friends, and observe what is just toward us, because of their good will toward us. We have confirmed therefore unto them the borders of Judaea, and also the three governments of Aphaerema and Lydda and Ramathaim (these were added unto Judaea from the country of Samaria), and all things appertaining unto them, for all such as do sacrifice in Jerusalem, instead of the king's dues which the king received of them yearly aforetime from the produce of the earth and the fruits of trees. And as for the other things that pertain unto us from henceforth, of the tenths and the tolls that pertain unto us, and the saltpits, and the crowns that pertain unto us, all these we will bestow upon them. And not one of these things shall be annulled from this time forth and for ever. Now therefore be careful to make a copy of these things, and let it be given unto Jonathan, and let it be set up on the holy mount in a meet and conspicuous place.

And king Demetrius saw that the land was quiet before him, and that no resistance was made to him, and he sent away all his forces, each man to his own place, except the foreign forces, which he had raised from the isles of the Gentiles: and all the forces of his fathers hated him. Now Tryphon was of those who aforetime had been of Alexander's part, and he saw that all the forces murmured against Demetrius, and he went to Imalcue the Arabian, who was nourishing up Antiochus the young child of Alexander, and pressed sore upon him that he should deliver him unto him, that he might reign in his father's stead: and he told him all that Demetrius had done, and the hatred wherewith his forces hated him; and he abode there many days.

And Jonathan sent unto king Demetrius, that he should cast out of Jerusalem them of the citadel, and them that were in the strongholds; for they fought against Israel continually. And Demetrius sent unto Jonathan, saying I will not only do this for thee and thy nation, but I will greatly honour thee and thy nation, if I find fair occasion. Now therefore thou shalt do well, if thou send me men who shall fight for me; for all my forces are revolted. And Jonathan sent him three thousand valiant men unto Antioch: and they came to the king, and the king was glad at their coming. And they of the city gathered themselves together into the midst of the city, to the number of a hundred and twenty thousand men, and they were minded to slay the king. And the king fled into the court of the palace, and they of the city seized the passages of the city, and began to fight. And the king called the Jews to help him, and they were gathered together unto him all at once, and they dispersed themselves in the city, and slew that day to the number of a hundred thousand. And they set the city on fire, and gat many spoils that day, and saved the king. And they of the city saw that the Jews had made them selves masters of the city as they would, and they waxed faint in their hearts, and they cried out to the king with supplication, saying, Give us thy right hand, and let the Jews cease from fighting against us and the city. And they cast away their arms, and made peace; and the Jews were glorified in the sight of the king, and before all that were in his kingdom; and they returned to Jerusalem, having many spoils. And king Demetrius sat on the throne of his kingdom, and the land was quiet before him. And he lied in all that he spake, and estranged himself from Jonathan, and recompensed him not according to the benefits with which he had recompensed him, and afflicted him exceedingly.

Now after this Tryphon returned, and with him the young child Antiochus; and he reigned, and put on a diadem. And there were gathered unto him all the forces which Demetrius had sent away with disgrace, and they fought against him, and he fled and was put to the rout. And Tryphon took the elephants, and became master of Antioch. And the young Antiochus wrote unto Jonathan, appoint thee over the four governments, and to be one of the king's Friends. And he sent unto him golden vessels and furniture for the table, and gave him leave to drink in golden vessels, and to be clothed in purple, and to have a golden buckle. And his brother Simon he made captain from the Ladder of Tyre unto the borders of Egypt. And Jonathan went forth, and took his journey beyond the river and through the cities; and all the forces of Syria gathered themselves unto him for to be his confederates. And he came to Ascalon, and they of the city met him honourably. And he departed thence to Gaza, and they of Gaza shut him out; and he laid siege unto it, and burned the suburbs thereof with fire, and spoiled them. And they of Gaza made request unto Jonathan, and he gave them his right hand, and took the sons of their princes for hostages, and sent them away to Jerusalem; and he passed through the country as far as Damascus.

And Jonathan heard that Demetrius' princes were come to Kedesh, which is in Galilee, with a great host, purposing to remove him from his office; and he went to meet them, but Simon his brother he left in the country. And Simon encamped against Bethsura, and fought against it many days, and shut it up: and they made request to him that he would give them his right hand, and he gave it to them; and he put them out from thence, and took possession of the city, and set a garrison over it. And Jonathan and his army encamped at the water of Gennesareth, and early in the morning they gat them to the plain of Hazor. And, behold, an army of strangers met him in the plain, and they laid an ambush for him in the mountains, but themselves met him face to face. But they that lay in ambush rose out of their places, and joined battle; and all they that were of Jonathan's side fled: not one of them was left, except Mattathias the son of Absalom, and Judas the son of Chalphi, captains of the forces. And Jonathan rent his clothes, and put earth upon his head, and prayed. And he turned again unto them in battle, and put them to the rout, and they fled. And they of his side that fled saw it, and returned unto him, and pursued with him unto Kedesh unto their camp, and they encamped there. And there fell of the strangers on that day about three thousand men: and Jonathan returned to Jerusalem.

CHAPTER XII

AND Jonathan saw that the time served him, and he chose men, and sent them to Rome, to confirm and renew the friendship that they had with them. And to the Spartans, and to other places, he sent letters after the same manner. And they went unto Rome, and entered into the senate house, and said, Jonathan the high priest, and the nation of the Jews, have sent us, to renew for them the friendship and the confederacy, as in former time. And they gave them letters unto the men in every place, that they should bring them on their way to the land of Judah in peace: And this is the copy of the letters which Jonathan wrote to the Spartans:

Jonathan the high priest, and the senate of the nation, and the priests, and the rest of the people of the Jews, unto their brethren the Spartans, greeting: Even before this time were letters sent unto Onias the high priest from Arius, who was reigning among you, to signify that ye are our brethren, as the copy here underwritten sheweth. And Onias entreated honourably the man that was sent, and received the letters, wherein declaration was made of confederacy and friendship. Therefore we also, albeit we need none of these things, having for our encouragement the holy books which are in our hands, have assayed to send that we might renew our brotherhood and friendship with you, to the end that we should not become estranged from you altogether: for all times without ceasing, both in our feasts, and on the other convenient days, do remember you in the sacrifices which we offer, and in our prayers, as it is right and meet to be mindful of brethren: and moreover are glad for your glory. But as for ourselves, many afflictions and many wars have encompassed us, and the kings that are round about us have fought against us. We were not minded therefore to be troublesome unto you, and to the rest of our confederates and friends, in these wars; for we have the help which is from heaven to help us, and we have been delivered from our enemies, and our enemies have been brought low. We chose therefore Numenius the son of Antiochus, and Antipater the son of Jason, and have sent them unto the Romans, to renew the friendship that we had with them, and the former confederacy. We commanded them therefore to go also unto you, and to salute you, and to deliver you our letters concerning the renewing of friendship and our brotherhood. And now ye shall do well if ye give us an answer thereto.

And this is the copy of the letters which they sent to Onias:

Arius king of the Spartans to Onias the chief priest, greeting: It hath been found in writing, concerning the Spartans and the Jews, that they are brethren, and that they are of the stock of Abraham: and now, since this is come to our knowledge, ye shall do well to write unto us of your prosperity. And we moreover do write on our part to you, that your cattle and goods are ours, and ours are yours. We do command therefore that they make report unto you on this wise.

And Jonathan heard that Demetrius' princes were returned to fight against him with a greater host than afore, and he removed from Jerusalem, and met them in the country of Hamath; for he gave them no respite to set foot in his country. And he sent spies into his camp, and they came again, and reported to him that they were appointed in such and such a way to fall upon them in the night season. But so soon as the sun was down, Jonathan commanded his men to watch, and to be in arms, that all the night long they might be ready for battle: and he put forth sentinels round about the camp. And the adversaries heard that Jonathan and his men were ready for battle, and they feared, and trembled in their hearts, and they kindled fires in their camp. But Jonathan and his men knew it not till the morning; for they saw the lights burning. And Jonathan pursued after them, and overtook them not; for they were gone over the river Eleutherus. And Jonathan turned aside to the Arabians, who are called Zabadaeans, and smote them, and took their spoils. And he set out from thence, and came to Damascus, and took his journey through all the country. And Simon went forth, and took his journey as far as Ascalon, and the strongholds that were near unto it And he turned aside to Joppa, and took possession of it; for he had heard that they were minded to deliver the stronghold unto the men of Demetrius; and he set a garrison there to keep it.

And Jonathan returned, and called the elders of the people together; and he took counsel with them to build strongholds in Judea, and to make the walls of Jerusalem higher, and to raise a great mound between the citadel and the city, for to separate it from the city, that so it might be all alone, that men might neither buy nor sell And they were gathered together to build the city, and there fell down part of the wall of the brook that is on the east side, and he repaired that which is called Chaphenathan. And Simon also built Adida in the plain country, and made it strong, and set up gates and bars.

And Tryphon sought to reign over Asia and to put on himself the diadem, and to stretch forth his hand against Antiochus the king. And he was afraid lest haply Jonathan should not suffer him, and lest he should fight against him; and he sought a way how to take him, that he might destroy him. And he removed, and came to Bethshan. And Jonathan came forth to meet him with forty thousand men chosen for battle, and came to Bethshan. And Tryphon saw that he came with a great host, and he was afraid to stretch forth his hand against him: and he received him honourably and commended him unto all his Friends, and gave him gifts, and commanded his forces to be obedient unto him, as unto himself. And he said unto Jonathan, Why hast thou put all this people to trouble, seeing there is no war betwixt us? And now send them away to their homes, but choose for thyself a few men who shall be with thee, and come thou with me to Ptolemais, and I will give it up to thee, and the rest of the strongholds and the rest of the forces, and all the king's officers: and I will return and depart; for this is the cause of my coming. And he put trust in him, and did even as he said, and sent away his forces, and they departed into the land of Judah. But he reserved to himself three thousand men, of whom he left two thousand in Galilee, but one thousand went with him. Now as soon as Jonathan entered into Ptolemais, they of Ptolemais shut the gates, and laid hands on him; and all them that came in with him they slew with the sword. And Tryphon sent forces and horsemen into Galilee, and into the great plain, to destroy all Jonathan's men. And they perceived that he was taken and had perished, and they that were with him; and they encouraged one another, and went on their way close together, prepared to fight. And they that followed upon them saw that they were ready to fight for their lives, and turned back again. And they all came in peace into the land of Judah, and they mourned for Jonathan, and them that were with him, and they were sore afraid; and all Israel mourned with great mourning. And all the Gentiles that were round about them sought to destroy them utterly: for they said, They have no ruler, nor any to help them: now therefore let us fight against them, and take away their memorial from among mẹn.

CHAPTER XIII

AND Simon heard that Tryphon had gathered together a mighty host to come into the land of Judah, and destroy it utterly. And he saw that the people trembled and was in great fear; and he went up to Jerusalem, and gathered the people together; and he encouraged them. and said unto them, Ye yourselves know all the things that I and my brethren, and my father's house, have done for the laws and the sanctuary, and the battles and the distresses which we have seen: by reason hereof all my brethren have perished for Israel's sake, and I am le% alone. And now be it far from me, that I should spare mine ow.n life in any time of affliction; for I am not better than my brethren. Howbeit I will take vengeance for my nation, and for the sanctuary, and for our wives and children; because all the Gentiles are gathered to destroy us of very hatred. And the spirit of the people revived, as soon as they heard these words. And they answered with a loud voice, saying, Ihou art our leader instead of Judas and Jonathan thy brother. Fight thou our battles, and all that thou shalt say unto us, that will we do. And he gathered together all the men of war, and made haste to finish the walls of Jerusalem, and he fortified it round about. And he sent Jonathan the son of Absalom, and with him a great host, to Joppa: and he cast out them that were therein, and abode there in it.

And Tryphon removed from Ptolemais with a mighty host to enter into the land of Judah, and Jonathan was with him in ward. But Simon encamped at Adida, over against the plain, And Tryphon knew that Simon was risen up instead of his brother Jonathan, and meant to join battle with him, and he sent ambassadors unto him, saying, It is for money which Jonathan thy brother owed unto the king's treasure, by reason of the offices which he had, that we hold him fast. And now send a hundred talents of silver, and two of his sons for hostages, that when he is set at liberty he may not revolt from us, and we will set him at liberty. And Simon knew that they spake unto him deceitfully; and he sendeth the money and the children, lest peradventure he should procure to himself great hatred of the people, and they should say, Because I sent him not the money and the children, he perished. And he sent the children and the hundred talents. And he dealt falsely, and did not set Jonathan at liberty. And after this Tryphon came to invade the land, and destroy it, and he went round about by the way that leadeth unto Adora: and Simon and his army marched over against him to every place, wheresoever he went. Now they of the citadel sent unto Tryphon ambassadors, hastening him to come unto them through the wilderness, and to send them victuals. And Tryphon made ready all his horse to come: and on that night there fell a very great snow, and he came not by reason of the snow. And he removed, and came into the country of Gilead. But when he came near to Bascama, he slew Jonathan, and he was buried there. And Tryphon returned, and went away into his own land.

And Simon sent, and took the bones of Jonathan his brother, and buried him at Modin, the city of his fathers. And all Israel made great lamentation over him, and mourned for him many days. And Simon built a monument upon the sepulchre of his father and his brethren, and raised it aloft to the sight, with polished stone behind and before. And he set up seven pyramids, one over against another, for his father, and his mother, and his four brethren. And for these he made cunning devices, setting about them great pillars, and upon the pillars he fashioned all manner of arms for a perpetual memory, and beside the arms ships carved, that they should be seen of all that sail on the sea. This is the sepulchre which he made at Modin, and it is there unto this day.

Now Tryphon dealt deceitfully with the young king Antiochus, and slew him, and reigned in his stead, and put on himself the diadem of Asia, and brought a great calamity upon the land. And Simon built the strongholds of Judaea, and fenced them about with high towers, and great walls, and gates, and bars; and he laid up victuals in the strongholds. And Simon chose men, and sent to king Demetrius, to the end he should give the country an immunity, because all that Tryphon did was to plunder. And king Demetrius sent unto him according to these words, and answered him, and wrote a letter unto him, after this manner:

King Demetrius unto Simon the high priest and Friend of kings, and unto the elders and nation of the Jews, greeting: The golden crown, and the palm branch, which ye sent, we have received: and we are ready to make a stedfast peace with you, yea, and to write unto our officers, to grant immunities unto you. And whatsoever things we confirmed unto you, they are confirmed; and the strongholds, which ye have builded, let them be your own. As for any oversights and faults committed unto this day, we forgive them, and the crown which ye owed us: and if there were any other toll exacted in Jerusalem, let it be exacted no longer. And if there be any among you meet to be enrolled in our court, let them be enrolled, and let there be peace betwixt us. In the hundred and seventieth year was the yoke of the heathen taken away from Israel. And the people began to write in their instruments and contracts, in the first y ear of Simon the great high priest and captain and leader of the Jews.

In those days he encamped against Gazara, and compassed it round about with armies; and he made an engine of siege, and brought it up to the city, and smote a tower, and took it. And they that were in the engine leaped forth into the city; and there was a great uproar in the city: and they of the city rent their clothes, and went up on the walls with their wives and children, and cried with a loud voice, making request to Simon to give them his right hand. And they said, Deal not with us according to our wickedness, but according to thy mercy. And Simon was reconciled unto them, and did not fight against them: and he put them out of the city, and cleansed the houses wherein the idols were, and so entered into it with singing and giving praise. And he put all uncleanness out of it, and placed in it such men as would keep the law, and made it stronger than it was before, and built therein a dwelling place for himself.

But they of the citadel in Jerusalem were hindered from going forth, and from going into the country, and from buying and selling; and they hungered exceedingly, and a great umber of them perished through famine. And they cried out to Simon, that he should give them his right hand; and he gave it to them: and he put them out from thence, and he cleansed the citadel from its pollutions. And he entered into it on the three and twentieth day of the second month, in the hundred and seventy and first year, with praise and palm branches, and with harps, and with cymbals, and with viols, and with hymns, and with songs: because a great enemy was destroyed out of Israel. And he ordained that they should keep that day every year with gladness. And the hill of the temple that was by the citadel he made stronger than before, and there he dwelt, himself and his men. And Simon was that John his son was valiant man, and he made him leader of all his forces: and he dwelt in Gazara.

CHAPTER XIV

AND in the hundred and seventy and second year king Demetrius gathered his forces together, and went into Media, to get him help, that he might fight against Tryphon. And Arsaces, the king of Persia and Media, heard that Demetrius was come into his borders, and he sent one of his princes to take him alive: and he went and smote the army of Demetrius, and took him, and brought him to Arsaces; and he put him in ward.

And the land had rest all the days of Simon: and he sought the good of his nation; and his authority and his glory was well-pleasing to them all his days. And amid all his glory he took Joppa for a haven, and made it an entrance for the isles of the sea; and he enlarged the borders of his nation, and gat possession of the country; and he gathered together a great number of captives, and gat the dominion of Gazara, and Bethsura, and the citadel, and he took away from it its uncleannesses; and there was none that resisted him. And they tilled their land in peace, and the land gave her increase, and the trees of the plains their fruit. The ancient men sat in the streets, they communed all of them together of good things, and the young men put on glorious and warlike apparel. He provided victuals for the cities, and furnished them with all manner of munition, until the name of his glory was named unto the end of the earth. He made peace in the land, and Israel rejoiced with great joy: and they sat each man under his vine and his fig tree, and there was none to make them afraid: and there ceased in the land any that fought against them: and the kings were discomfited in those days. And he strengthened all those of his people that were brought low: the law he searched out, and every lawless and wicked person he took away. He glorified the sanctuary, and the vessels of the temple he multiplied.

And it was heard at Rome that Jonathan was dead, and even unto Sparta, and they were exceeding sorry. But as soon as they heard that his brother Simon was made high priest in his stead, and ruled the country, and the cities therein, they wrote unto him on tables of brass, to renew with him the friendship and the confederacy which they had confirmed with Judas and Jonathan his brethren; and they were read before the congregation at Jerusalem. And this is the copy of the letters which the Spartans sent:

The rulers of the Spartans, and the city, unto Simon the high priest, and unto the elders, and the priests, and the residue of the people of the Jews, our brethren, greeting: The ambassadors that were sent unto our people made report to us of your glory and honour: and we were glad for their coming, and we did register the things that were spoken by them in the public records after this manner: Numenius son of Antiochus, and Antipater son of Jason, the Jews' ambassadors, came unto us to renew the friendship they had with us. And it pleased the people to entertain the men honourably, and to put the copy of their words in the public records, to the end that the people of the Spartans might have a memorial thereof: moreover they wrote a copy of these things unto Simon the high priest.

After this Simon sent Numenius to Rome with a great shield of gold of a thousand pound weight, in order to confirm the confederacy with them.

But when the people heard these things, they said, What thanks shall we give to Simon and his sons? for he and his brethren and the house of his father have made themselves strong, and have chased away in fight the enemies of Israel from them, and confirmed liberty to Israel. And they wrote on tables, of brass, and set them upon pillars in mount Sion: and this is the copy of the writing:

On the eighteenth day of Elul, in the hundred and seventy and second year, and this is the third year of Simon the high priest, in Asaramel, in a great congregation of priests and people and princes of the nation, and of the elders of the country, was it notified unto us: Forasmuch as oftentimes there have been wars in the country, but Simon the son of Mattathias, the son of the sons of Joarib, and the brethren, put themselves in jeopardy, and withstood the enemies of their nation, that their sanctuary and the law might be established, and glorified their nation with great glory: and Jonathan assembled their nation together, and became their high priest, and was gathered to his people: and their enemies purposed to invade their country, that they might destroy their country utterly, and stretch forth their hands against their sanctuary: then rose up Simon, and fought for his nation, and spent much of his own substance, and armed the valiant men of his nation, and gave them wages: and he fortified the cities of Judea, and Bethsura that lieth upon the borders of Judea, where the arms of the enemies were afortime, and set there a garrison of Jews: and he fortified Joppa which is upon the sea, and Gazara which upon the border of Azotus, wherein the enemies dwelt afortime, and placed Jews there, and set therein all things convenient for the reparation thereof: and the people saw the faith of Simon, and the glory which he thought to bring unto his nation, and they made him their leader and high priest, because he had done all these things, and for the justice and the faith which he kept to his nation, and for that he sought by all means to exalt his people: and in his days things prospered in his hands, so that the Gentiles were taken away out of their country, and they also that were in the city of David, they that were in Jerusalem, who had made themselves a citadel, out of which they issued, and polluted all things round about the sanctuary, and did great hurt unto its purity; and he placed Jews therein, and fortified it for the safety of the country and the city, and made high the walls of Jerusalem: and king Demetrius confirmed to him the high priesthood according to these things, and made him one of his Friends, and honoured him with great honour; for he had heard say, that the Jews had been called by the Romans friends and confederates and brethren, and that they had met the ammbassadors of Simon honourably; and that the Jews and the priests were well pleased that Simon should be their leader and high priest for ever, until there should arise a faithful prophet; and that he should be captain over them, and should take charge of the sanctuary, to set them over their works, and over the country, and over the arms, and over the strongholds; and that he should take charge of the sanctuary, and that he should be obeyed by all, and that all instruments in the country should be written in his name, and that he should be clothed in purple, and wear gold; and that it should not be lawful for any of the people or of the priests to set at nought any of these things, or to gainsay the words that he should speak, or to gather an assembly in the country without him, or to be clothed in purple, or wear a buckle of gold; but whosoever should do otherwise, or set at nought any of these things, he should be liable to punishment. All the people consented to ordain for Simon that he should do according to these words; and Simon accepted hereof, and consented to be high priest, and to be captain and governor of the Jews and of the priests, and to be protector of all.

And they commanded to put this writing on tables of brass, and to set them up within the precinct of the sanctuary in a conspicuous place; and moreover to put the copies thereof in the treasury, to the end that Simon and his sons might have them.

CHAPTER XV

AND Antiochus son of Demetrius the king sent letters from the isles of the sea unto Simon the priest and governor of the Jews, and to all the nation; and the contents thereof were after thiS manner:

King Antiochus to Simon the chief priest and governor, and to the nation of the Jews, greeting: Forasmuch as certain pestilent fellows have made themselves masters of the kingdom of our fathers, but my purpose is to claim the kingdom, that I may restore it as it was before; and moreover I have raised a multitude of foreign soldiers, and have prepared ships of war; moreover I am minded to land in the country that I may punish them that have destroyed our country, and them that have made many cities in the kingdom desolate: Now therefore I confirm unto thee all the exactions which the kings that were before me remitted unto thee: and whatsoever gifts besides they remitted unto thee: and I give thee leave to coin money for they county with thine own stamp, but that Jerusalem and the sanctuary should be free: and all the arms that thou hast prepared, and the strongholds that thou hast built, which thou hast in thy possession, let them remain unto thee: and everything owing to the king, and the things that shall be owing to the king from henceforth and for evermore, let them be remitted unto thee: moreover, when we shall have established our kingdom, we will glorify thee and thy nation and the temple with great glory, so that your glory shall be made manifest in all the earth.

In the hundred and seventy and fourth year went Antiochus forth into the land of his fathers; and all the forces came together unto him, so that there were few men with Tryphon. And king Antiochus pursued him, and he came, as he fled, unto Dor, which is by the sea: for he knew that troubles were come upon him all at once, and that his forces had forsaken him. And Antiochus encamped against Dor, and with him a hundred and twenty thousand men of war, and eight thousand horse. And he compassed the city round about, and the ships joined in the attack from the sea; and he vexed the city by land and sea, and suffered no man to go out or in.

And Numenius and his company came from Rome, having letters to the kings and to the countries, wherein were written these things:

Lucius, consul of the Romans, unto king Ptolemy, greeting: The Jews' ambassador came unto us as our friends and confederates, to renew the old friendship and confederacy, being sent from Simon the high priest, and from the people of the Jews; moreover they brought a shield of gold of a thousand pound. It pleased us therefore to write unto the kings and unto the countries, that they should not seek their hurt, nor fight against them, and their cities, and their country, nor be confederates with such as fight against them. Moreover it seemed good to us to receive the shield of them. If therefore any pestilent fellows have fled from their country unto you, deliver them unto Simon the high priest, that he may take vengeance on them according to their law.

And the same things wrote he to Demetrius the king, and to Attalus, and to Arathes, and to Arsaces , and unto all the countries, and to Sampsames, and to the Spartans, and unto Delos, and unto Myndos, and unto Sicyon, and unto Caria, and unto Samos, and unto Pamphylia, and unto Lycia, and unto Halicarnassus, and unto Rhodes, and unto Phaselis, and unto Cos, and unto Side, and unto Aradus, and Gortyna, and Cnidus, and Cyprus, and Cyrene. But the copy hereof they wrote to Simon the high priest.

But Antiochus the king encamped against Dor the second day, bringing his forces up to it continually, and making engines of war, and he shut up Tryphon from going in or out. And Simon sent him two thousand chosen men to fight on his side; and silver, and gold, and instruments of war in abundance. And he would not receive them, but set at nought all the covenants which he had made with him aforetime, and was estranged from him. And he sent unto him Athenobius, one of his Friends, to commune with him, saying,

Ye hold possession of Joppa and Gazara, and the citadel that is in Jerusalem, cities of my kingdom. The borders thereof ye have wasted, and done great hurt in the land, and got the dominion of many places in my kingdom. Now therefore deliver up the cities which ye have taken, and the tributes of the places whereof ye have gotten dominion without the borders of Judaea: or else give me for them five hundred talents of silver; and for the harm that ye have done, and the tributes of the cities, other five hundred talents: or else we will come and subdue you.

And Athenobius the king's Friend came to Jerusalem; and he saw the glory of Simon, and the cupboard of gold and silver vessels, and his great attendance, and he was amazed; and he reported to him the king's words. And Simon answered, and said unto him,

We have neither taken other men's land, nor have we possession of that which appertaineth to others, but of the inheritance of our fathers; howbeit, it was had in possession of our enemies wrongfully for a certain time. But we, having opportunity, hold fast the inheritance of our fathers. But as touching Joppa and Gazara, which thou demandest, they did great harm among the people throughout our country, we will give a hundred talents for them.

And he answered him not a word, but returned in a rage to the king, and reported unto him these words, and the glory of Simon, and all that he had seen: and the king was exceeding wroth. But Tryphon embarked on board a ship, and fled to Orthosia.

And the king appointed Cendebaeus chief captain of the sea coast, and gave him forces of foot and horse: and he commanded him to encamp before Judaea, and he commanded him to build up Kidron, and to fortify the gates, and that he should fight against the people: but the king pursued Tryphon. And Cendebaeus came to Jamnia, and began to provoke the people, and to invade Judaea, and to take the people captive, and to slay them. And he built Kidron, and set horsemen there, and forces of foot, to the end that issuing out they might make outroads upon the ways of Judaea, according as the king commanded him.

CHAPTER XVI

AND John went up from Gazara, and told Simon his father what Cendebaeus was doing. And Simon called his two eldest sons, Judas and John, and said unto them, I and my brethren and my father's house have fought the battles of Israel from our youth, even unto this day; and things have prospered in our hands, that we should deliver Israel oftentimes. But now I am old, and ye moreover, by his mercy, are of a sufficient age: be ye instead of me and my brother, and go forth and fight for our nation; but let the help which is from heaven be with you. And he chose out of the country twenty thousand men of war and horsemen, and they went against Cendebaeus, and slept at Modin. And rising up in the morning, they went into the plain, and, behold, a great host came to meet them, of footmen and horsemen: and there was a brook betwixt them. And he encamped over against them, he and his people: and he saw that the people were afraid to pass over the brook, and he passed over first, and the men saw him, and passed over after him. And he divided the people, and set the horsemen in the midst of the footmen: but the enemies' horsemen were exceeding many. And they sounded with the trumpets; and Cendebaeus and his army were put to the rout, and there fell of them many wounded to death, but they that were left fled to the stronghold: at that time was Judas John's brother wounded: but John pursued after them, till he came unto Kidron, which Cendebaeus had built; and they fled unto the towers that are in the fields of Azotus; and he burned it with fire; and there fell of them about two thousand men. And he returned into Judaea in peace.

And Ptolemy the son of Abubus had been appointed captain for the plain of Jericho, and he had much silver and gold; for he was the high priest's son in law. And his heart was lifted up, and he was minded to make himself master of the country, and he took counsel deceitfully against Simon and his sons, to make away with them. Now Simon was visiting the cities that were in the country, and taking care for the good ordering of them; and he went down to Jericho, himself and Mattathias and Judas his sons, in the hundred and seventy and seventh year, in the eleventh month, the same is the month Sebat: and the son of Abubus received them deceitfully into the little stronghold that is called Dok, which he had built, and made them a great banquet, and hid men there. And when Simon and his sons had drunk freely, Ptolemy and his men rose up, and took their arms, and came in upon Simon into the banqueting place, and slew him, and his two sons, and certain of his servants. And he committed a great iniquity, and recompensed evil for good. And Ptolemy wrote these things, and sent to the king, that he should send him forces to aid him, and should deliver him their country and the cities. And he sent others to Gazara to make away with John: and unto the captains of thousands he sent letters to come unto him, that he might give them silver and gold and gifts. And others he sent to take possession of Jerusalem, and the mount of the temple. And one ran before to Gazara, and told John that his father and brethren were perished, and he hath sent to slay thee also. And when he heard, he was sore amazed; and he laid hands on the men that came to destroy him, and slew them; for he perceived that they were seeking to destroy him.

And the rest of the acts of John, and of his wars, and of his valiant deeds which he did, and of the building of thd walls which he had built, and of his doings, behold, they are written in the chronicles of his high priesthood, from the time that he was made high priest after his father.

2 MACCABEES

(FIRST CENTURY A.D.)

A NEW TRANSLATION AND INTRODUCTION
BY H. ANDERSON

The brethren, the Jews that are in Jerusalem and they that are in the country of Judaea, send greeting to the brethren, the Jews that are throughout Egypt, and wish them good peace: and may God do good unto you, and remember his covenant with Abraham and Isaac and Jacob, his faithful servants; and give you all a heart to worship him and do his pleasure with a great heart and a willing soul; and open your heart in his law and in his statutes, and make peace, and hearken to your supplications, and be reconciled with you, and not forsake you in an evil time. And now we here are praying for you. In the reign of Demetrius, in the hundred three score and ninth year, we the Jews have already written unto you in the tribulation and in the extremity that hath come upon us in these years, from the time that Jason and his company revolted from the holy land and the kingdom, and set the gate on fire, and shed innocent blood: and we besought the Lord, and were heard; and we offered sacrifice and meal offering, and we lighted the lamps, and we set forth the shewbread. And now see that ye keep the days of the feast of tabernacles of the month Chislev. Written in the hundred fourscore and eighth year.

They that are in Jerusalem and they that are in Judaea and the senate and Judas, unto Aristobulus, king Ptolemy's teacher, who is also of the stock of the anointed priests, and unto the Jews that are in Egypt, send greeting and health. Having been saved by God out of great perils, as men arrayed against a king, we thank him greatly. For himself cast forth into Persia them that arrayed themselves against us in the holy city. For when the prince was come there, and the army with him that seemed irresistible, they were cut to pieces in the temple of Nanaea by the treachery of Nanaea's priests. For Antiochus, on the pretence that he would marry her, came into the place, he and his Friends that were with him, that they might take a great part of the treasures in name of a dowry. And when the priests of Nanaea's temple had set the treasures forth, and he was come there with a small company within the wall of the precincts, they shut to the temple when Antiochus was come in: and opening the secret door of the panelled ceiling, they threw stones and struck down the prince, and they hewed him and his company in pieces, and smote off their heads, and cast them to those that were without. Blessed be our God in all things, who gave for a prey them that had committed impiety.

Whereas we are now about to keep the purification of the temple in the month Chislev, on the five and twentieth day, we thought it necessary to certify you thereof, that ye also may keep a feast of tabernacles, and a memorial of the fire which was given when Nehemiah offered sacrifices, after that he had builded both the temple and the altar. For indeed when our fathers were about to be led into the land of Persia, the godly priests of that time took of the fire of the altar, and hid it privily in the hollow of a well that was without water, wherein they made it sure, so that the place was unknown to all men. Now after many years, when it pleased God, Nehemiah, having received a charge from the king of Persia, sent in quest of the fire the descendants of the priests that hid it. When they declared to us that they had found no fire, but thick water, he commanded them to draw out thereof and bring to him: and when the sacrifices had been offered on the altar, Nehemiah commanded the priests to sprinkle with the water both the wood and the things laid thereupon. And when it was done, and some time had passed, and the sun shone out, which before was hid with clouds, there was kindled a great blaze, so that all men marvelled. And the priests made a prayer while the sacrifice was consuming, both the priests and all others, Jonathan leading and the rest answering, as Nehemiah did. And the prayer was after this manner:

O Lord, Lord God, the Creator of all things, who art terrible and strong and righteous and merciful, who alone art King and gracious, who alone suppliest every need, who alone art righteous and almighty and eternal, thou that savest Israel out of all evil, who madest the fathers thy chosen, and didst sanctify them: accept the sacrifice for all thy people Israel, and guard thine own portion, and consecrate it. Gather together our Dispersion, set at liberty them that are in bondage among the heathen, look upon them that are despised and abhorred, and let the heathen know that thou art our God. Torment them that oppress us and in arrogancy shamefully entreat us. Plant thy people in thy holy place, even as Moses said.

And thereupon the priests sang the hymns. And as soon as the sacrifice was consumed, then Nehemiah commanded to pour on great stones the water that was left. And when this was done, a flame was kindled; but when the light from the altar shone over against it, all was consumed. And when the matter became known, and it was told the king of the Persians, that, in the place where the priests that were led away had hid the fire, there appeared the water, wherewith also Nehemiah and they that were with him purified the sacrifice, then the king, inclosing the place, made it sacred, after he had proved the matter. And when the king would shew favour to any, he would take from them many presents and give them some of this water. And Nehemiah and they that were with him called this thing Nephthar, which is by interpretation, Cleansing; but most men call it Nephthai.

CHAPTER II

IT is also found in the records, that Jeremiah the prophet commanded them that were carried away to take of the fire, as hath been signified above: and how that the prophet charged them that were carried away, having given them the law, that they should not forget the statutes of the Lord, neither be led astray in their minds, when they saw images of gold and silver, and the adornmen thereof. And with other such words exhorted he them, that the law should not depart from their heart. And it was contained in the writing, that the prophet, being warned of God, commanded that the tabernacle and the ark should follow with him, when he went forth into the mountain where Moses went up and beheld the heritage of God. And Jeremiah came and found a chamber in the rock, and there he brought in the tabernacle, and the ark, and the altar of incense; and he made fast the door. And some of those that followeth witll him came there that they might mark the way, and could not find it. But when Jeremiah perceived it, he blamed them, saying, Yea and the place shall be unknown until God gather the people again together, and mercy come: and then shall the Lord disclose these things, and the glory of the Lord shall be seen, and the cloud.

As also it was shewed with Moses; as also Solomon besought that the place might be consecrated greatly, and it was also declared that he, having wisdom, offered a sacrifice of dedication, and of the finishing of the temple; so we would have it now. As Moses prayed unto the Lord, and fire came down out of heaven and consumed the sacrifice, even so prayed Solomon also, and the fire came down and consumed the burnt offerings; (and Moses said, Because the sin offering had not been eaten, it was consumed in like manner with the rest;) and Solomon kept the eight days.

And the same things were related both in the public archives and in the records that concern Nehemiah; and how he, founding a library, gathered together the books about the kings and prophets, and the books of David, and letters of kings about sacred gifts. And in like manner Judas also gathered together for us all those writings that had been scattered by reason of the war that befell, and they are still with us. If therefore ye have need thereof, send some to fetch them unto you.

Seeing then that we are about to keep the purification, we write unto you; ye will therefore do well if ye keep the days. Now God, who saved all his people, and restored the heritage to all, and the kingdom, and the priesthood, and the hallowing, even as he promised through the law, — in God have we hope, that he will quickly have mercy upon us, and gather us together out of all the earth into the holy place: for he delivered us out of great evils, and purified the place.

Now the things concerning Judas Maccabaeus and his brethren, and the purification of the great temple, and the dedication of the altar, and further the wars against Antiochus Epiphanes, and Eupator his son, and the manifestations that came from heaven unto those that vied with one another in manful deeds for the religion of the Jews; so that, being but a few, they rescued the whole country, and chased the barbarous multitudes, and recovered again the temple renowned all the world over, and freed the city, and restored the laws which were like to be overthrown, seeing the Lord became gracious unto them with all forbearance: these things, I say, which have been declared by Jason of Cyrene in five books, we will assay to abridge in one work. For having in view the confused mass of the numbers, and the difficulty which awaiteth them that would enter into the narratives of the history, by reason of the abundance of the matter, we were careful that they who choose to read may be attracted, and that they who wish well to our cause may find it easy to recall what we have written, and that all reader may have profit. And although to us, who have taken upon us the painful labour of the abridgement, the task is not easy, but a matter of sweat and watching (even as it is no light thing unto him that prepareth a banquet, and seeketh the benefit of others); yet for the sake of the gratitude of the many we will gladly endure the painful labour, leaving to the historian the exact handling of every particular, and again having no strength to fill in the outlines of our abridgement. For as the masterbuilder of a new house must care for the whole structure, and again he that undertaketh to decorate and paint it must seek out the things fit for the adorning thereof; even so I think it is also with us. To occupy the ground, and to indulge in long discussions, and to be curious in particulars, becometh the first author of the history: but to strive after brevity of expression, and to avoid a laboured fulness in the treatment, is to be granted to him that would bring a writing into a new form. Here then let us begin the narration, only adding thus much to that which hath been already said; for it is a foolish thing to make a long prologue to the history, and to abridge the history itself.

CHAPTER III

WHEN the holy city was inhabited with all peace, and the laws were kept very well, because of the godliness of Onias the high priest, and his hatred of wickedness, it came to pass that even the kings themselves did honour the place and glorify the temple with the noblest presents; insomuch that even Seleucus the king of Asia of his own revenues bare all the cost belonging to the services of the sacrifices.

But one Simon of the tribe of Benjamin, having been made guardian of the temple, fell out with the high priest about the ruling of the market in the city. And when he could not overcome Onias, he gat him to Apollonius the son of Thrasaeus, who at that time was governor of Coelesyria and Phoenicia: and he brought him word how that the treasury in Jerusalem was full of untold sums of money, so that the multitude of the funds was innumerable, and that they did not pertain to the account of the sacrifices, but that it was possible that these should fall under the king's power. And when Apollonius met the king, he informed him of the money whereof he had been told; and the king appointed Heliodorus, who was his chancellor, and sent him with a commandment to accomplish the removal of the aforesaid money. So forthwith Heliodorus took his journey, under a colour of visiting the cities of Coelesyria and Phoenicia, but in fact to execute the king's purpose. And when he was come to Jerusalem, and had been courteously reccived by the high priest of the city, he laid before them an account of the information which had been given him, and declared wherefore he was come; and he inquired if in truth these things were so. And the high priest explained to him that there were in the treasury deposits of widows and orphans, and moreover some money belonging to Hyrcanus the son of Tobias, a man in very high place, and that the case was not as that impious Simon falsely alleged; and that in all there were four hundred talents of silver and two hundred of gold; and that it was altogether impossible that wrong should be done unto them that had put trust in the holiness of the place, and in the majesty and inviolable sanctity of the temple, honoured over all the world. But Heliodorus, because of the king's commandments given him, said that in any case this money must be confiscated for the king's treasury.

So having appointed a day, he entered in to direct

the inquiry concerning these matters; and there was no small distress throughout the whole city. And the priests, prostrating themselves before the altar in their priestly garments, and looking toward heaven, called upon him that gave the law concerning deposits, that he should preserve these treasures safe for those that had deposited them. And whosoever saw the mien of the high priest was wounded in mind; for his countenance and the change of his colour betrayed the distress of his soul. For a terror and a shuddering of the body had come over the man, whereby the pain that was in his heart was plainly shewn to them that looked upon him. And they that were in the houses rushed flocking out to make a universal supplication, because the place was like to come into contempt. And the women, girt with sackcloth under their breasts, thronged the streets, and the virgins that were kept in ward ran together, some to the gates, others to the walls, and some looked out through the windows. And all, stretching forth their hands toward heaven, made their solemn supplication. Then it would have pitied a man to see the multitude prostrating themselves all mingled together, and the expectation of the high priest in his sore distress.

While therefore they called upon the Almighty Lord to keep the things intrusted to them safe and sure for those that had intrusted them, Heliodorus went on to execute that which had been decreed. But when he was already present there with his guards over against the treasury, the Sovereign of spirits and of all authority caused a great apparition, so that all that had presumed to come in with him, stricken with dismay at the power of God, fainted and were sore afraid. For there was seen by them a horse with a terrible rider upon him, and adorned with beautiful trappings, and he rushed fiercely and smote at Heliodorus with his forefeet, and it seemed that he that sat upon the horse had complete armour of gold. Two other also appeared unto him, young men notable in their strength, and beautiful in their glory, and splendid in their apparel, who stood by him on either side, and scourged him unceasingly, inflicting on him many sore stripes. And when he had fallen suddenly unto the ground, and great darkness had come over him, his guards caught him up and put him into a litter, and carried him, him that had just now entered with a great train and all his guard into the aforesaid treasury, himself now brought to utter helplessness, manifestly made to recognise the sovereignty of God. And so, while he, through the working of God, speechless and bereft of all hope and deliverance, lay prostrate, they blessed the Lord, that made marvellous his own place; and the temple, which a little afore was full of terror and alarm, was filled with joy and gladness after the Almighty Lord appeared.

But quickly certain of Heliodorus's familiar friends besought Onias to call upon the Most High, and grant life to him who lay quite at the last gasp. And the high priest, secretly fearing lest the king might come to think that some treachery toward Heliodorus had been perpetrated by the Jews, brought a sacrifice for the deliverance of the man. But as the high priest was making the propitiation, the same young men appeared again to Heliodorus, arrayed in the same garments; and they stood and said, Give Onias the high priest great thanks, for his sake the Lord hath granted thee life; and do thou, since thou hast been scourged from heaven, publish unto all men the sovereign majesty of God. And when they had spoken these words, they vanished out of sight. So Heliodorus, having offered a sacrifice unto the Lord and vowed great vows unto him that had saved his life, and having graciously received Onias, returned with his host to the king. And he testified to all men the works of the great God which he had beheld with his eyes.

And when the king asked Heliodorus, what manner of man was fit to be sent yet once again to Jerusalem, he said, If thou hast any enemy or conspirator against the state, send him thither, and thou shalt receive him back well scourged, if he even escape with his life; because of a truth there is about the place a power of God. For he that hath his dwelling in heaven himself hath his eyes upon that place, and helpeth it; and them that come to hurt it he smiteth and destroyeth.

And such was the history of Heliodorus and the keeping of the treasury.

CHAPTER IV

BUT the aforesaid Simon, he who had given information of the money, and had betrayed his country, slandered Onias, saying that it was he who had incited Heliodorus, and made himself the author of these evils. And him that was the benefactor of the city, and the guardian of his fellow - countrymen, and a zealot for the laws, he dared to call a conspirator against the state. But when the growing enmity between them waxed so great, that even murders were perpetrated through one of Simon's trusted followers, Onias, seeing the danger of the contention and that Apollonius the son of Menestheus, the governor of Coelesyria and Phoenicia, was increasing Simon's malice, betook himself to the king, not to be an accuser of his fellow-citizens, but looking to the good of all the people, both public and private; for he saw that without the king's providence it was impossible for the state to obtain peace any more, and that Simon would not cease from his madness.

But when Seleucus was deceased, and Antiochus, who was called Epiphanes, succeeded to the kingdom, Jason the brother of Onias supplanted his brother in the high priesthood, having promised unto the king at an audience three hundred and threescore talents of silver, and out of another fund eighty talents; and beside this, he under took to assign a hundred and fifty more, if it might be allowed him through the king's authority to set him up a Greek place of exercise and form a body of youths to be trained therein, and to register the inhabitants of Jerusalem as citizens of Antioch. And when the king had given assent, and he had gotten possession of the office, he forthwith brought over them of his own race to the Greek fashion. And setting aside the royal ordinances of special favour to the Jews, granted by the means of John the father of Eupolemus, who went on the ambassage to the Romans for friendship and alliance, and seeking to overthrow the lawful modes of life, he brought in new customs forbidden by the law: for he eagerly established a Greek place of exercise under the citadel itself; and caused the noblest of the young men to wear the Greek cap. And thus there was an extreme of Greek fashions, and an advance of an alien religion, by reason of the exceeding profaneness of Jason, that ungodly man and no high priest; so that the priests had no more any zeal for the services of the altar: but despising the sanctuary, and neglecting the sacrifices, they hastened to enjoy that which was unlawfully provided in the palaestra, after the summons of the discus; making of no account the honours of their fathers, and thinking the glories of the Greeks best of all. By reason whereof sore calamity beset them; and the men whose ways of living they earnestly followed, and unto whom they desired to be made like in all things, these they had to be their enemies and to punish them. For it is not a light thing to do impiously against the laws of God: but these things the time following shall declare.

Now when certain games that came every fifth year were kept at Tyre, and the king was present, the vile Jason sent sacred envoys, as being Antiochians of Jerusalem, bearing three hundred drachmas of silver to the sacrifice of Hercules, which even the bearers thereof thought not right to use for any sacrifice, because it was not fit, but to expand on another charge. And though in the purpose of the sender this money was for the sacrifice of Hercules, yet on account of present circumstances it went to the equipment of the galleys. Now when Apollonius the son of Menestheus was sent into Egypt for the enthronement of Ptolemy Philometor as king, Antiochus, learning that Ptolemy has shewn himself ill affected toward his state, took thought for the security of his realm; wherefore, going by sea to Joppa, he travelled on to Jerusalem. And being magnificently received by Jason and the city, he was brought in with torches and shoutings. This done, he afterward led his army down into Phoenicia.

Now after a space of three years Jason sent Menelaus, the aforesaid Simon's brother, to bear the money unto the king, and to make reports concerning some neccssary matters. But he being commended to the king, and having glorified himself by the display of his authority, got the high priesthood for himself; outbidding Jason by three hundred talents of silver. And having received the royal mandates he came to Jerusalem, bringing nothing worthy the high priesthood, but having the passion of a cruel tyrant, and the rage of a savage beast. And whereas Jason, who had supplanted his own brother, was supplanted by another and driven as a fugitive into the country of the Ammonites, Menelaus had possession of the office: but of the money that had been promised to the king nothing was duly paid, and that though Sostratus the governor of the citadel demanded it (for unto him appertained the gathering of the revenues); for which cause they were both called by the king to his presence. And Menelaus left his own brother Lysimachus for his deputy in the high priesthood; and Sostratus left Crates, who was over the Cyprians.

Now while such was the state of things, it came to pass that they of Tarsus and Mallus made insurrection, because they were to be given as a present to Antiochis, the king's concubine. The king therefore came to Cilicia in all haste to settle matters, leaving for his deputy Andronicus, a man of high rank. And Menelaus, supposing that he had gotten a favourable opportunity, presented to Andronicus certain vessels of gold belonging to the temple, which he had stolen: other vessels also he had already sold into Tyre and the cities round about. And when Onias had sure knowledge of this, he sharply reproved him, having withdrawn himself into a sanctuary at Daphne, that lieth by Antioch. Wherefore Menelaus, taking Andronicus apart, prayed him to kill Onias. And coming to Onias, and being persuaded to use treachery, and being received as a friend, Andronicus gave him his right hand with oaths of fidelity, and, though he was suspected by him, so persuaded him to come forth of the sanctuary; and forthwith he despatched him without regard of justice. For the which cause not only Jews, but many also of the other nations, had indignation and displeasure at the unjust murder of the man. And when the king was come back again from the places in Cilicia, the Jews that were in the city pleaded before him against Andronicus (the Greeks also joining with them in hatred of the wickedness), urging that Onias had been wrongfully slain. Antiochus therefore was heartily sorry, and was moved to pity, and wept, because of the sober and well ordered life of him that was dead; and being inflamed with passion, forthwith he stripped off Andronicus's purple robe, and rent off his under garments, and when he had led him round through the whole city unto that very place where he had committed impiety against Onias, there he put the murderer out of the way, the Lord rendering to him the punishment he had deserved.

Now when many sacrileges had been committed in the city by Lysinachus with the consent of Menelaus, and when the bruit thereof was spread abroad outside, the people gathered themselves together against Lysimachus, after many vessels of gold had been already dispersed. And when the multitudes were rising against him, and were filled with anger, Lysimachus armed about three thousand men, and with unrighteous violence began the conflict, one Hauran, a man far gone in year and no less also in madness, leading the attack. But when they perceived the assault of Lysimachus, some caught up stones, others logs of wood, and some took handfuls of the ashes that lay near, and they flung them all pell-mell upon Lysimachus and them that were with him; by reason of which they wounded many of them, and some they struck to the ground, and all of them they forced to flee, but the author of the sacrilege himself they killed beside the treasury.

But touching these matters there was an accusation laid against Menelaus. And when the king was come to Tyre, the three men that were sent by the senate pleaded the cause before him. But Menelaus, seeing himself now defeated, promised much money to Ptolemy the son of Dorymenes, that he might win over the king. Whereupon Ptolemy taking the king aside into a cloister, as it were to take the air, brought him to be of another mind: and him that was the cause of all the evil, Menelaus, he discharged from the accusations; but those hapless men, who, if they had pleaded even before Scythians, would have been discharged uncondemned, them he sentenced to death. Soon then did they that were spokesmen for the city and the families of Israel and the holy vessels suffer that unrighteous penalty. For which cause even certain Tyrians, moved with hatred of the wickedness, provided magnificently for their burial. But Menelaus through the covetous dealings of them that were in power remained still in his office, cleaving to wickedness, as a great conspirator against his fellow-citizens.

CHAPTER V

NOW about this time Antiochus made his second inroad into Egypt. And it so befell that throughout all the city, for the space of almost forty days, there appeared in the midst of the sky horsemen in swift motion, wearing robes inwrought with gold and carrying spears, equipped in troops for battle; and drawing of swords; and on the other side squadrons of horse in array; and encounters and pursuits of both armies; and shaking of shields, and multitudes of lances, and casting of darts, and flashing of golden trappings, and girding on of all sorts of armour. Wherefore all men besought that the vision might have been given for good.

But when a false rumour had arisen that Antiochus was deceased, Jason took not less than a thousand men, and suddenly made an assault upon the city; and they that were upon the wall being routed, and the city being now at length well nigh taken, Menelaus took refuge in the citadel. But Jason slaughtered his own citizens without mercy, not considering that good success against kinsmen is the greatest ill success, but supposing himself to be setting up trophies over enemies, and not over fellow countrymen. The office however he did not get, but, receiving shame as the end of his conspiracy, he passed again a fugitive into the county of the Ammonites. At the last therefore he met with a miserable end: having been shut up at the court of Aretas the prince of the Arabians, fleeing from city to city, pursued of all men, hated as an apostate from the laws, and held in abomination as the butcher of his country and his fellow-citizens, he was cast forth into Egypt; and he that had driven many from their own country into strange lands perished himself in a strange land, having crossed the sea to the Lacedaemonians, as thinking to find shelter there because they were near of kin; and he that had cast out a multitude unburied had none to mourn for him, nor had he any funeral at all, or place in the sepulchre of his fathers.

Now when tidings came to the king concerning that which was done, he thought that Judaea was in revolt; whereupon setting out from Egypt in a furious mind, he took the city by force of arms, and commanded his soldiers to cut down without mercy such as came in their way, and to slay such as went up upon the houses; and there was killing of young and old, making away of boys, women, and children, slaying of virgins and infants. And in all the three days of the slaughter there were destroyed fourscore thousand, whereof forty thousand were slain in close combat, and no fewer were sold than slain. But not content with this he presumed to enter into the most holy temple of all the earth, having Menelaus for his guide (him that had proved himself a traitor both to the laws and to his country), even taking the sacred vessels with his polluted hands, and dragging down with his profane hands the offerings that had been dedicated by other kings to the augmentation and glory and honour of the place. And Antiochus was lifted up in mind, not seeing that because of the sins of them that dwelt in the city the Sovereign Lord had been provoked to anger a little while, and therefore his eye was then turned away from the place. But had it not so been that they were already holden by many sins, this man, even as Heliodorus who was sent by Seleucus the king to view the treasury, would, so soon as he pressed forward, have been scourged and turned back from his daring deed. Howbeit the Lord did not choose the nation for the place's sake, but the place for the nation's sake. Wherefore also the place itself, having partaken in the calamities that befell the nation, did afterward share in its benefits; and the place which was forsaken in the wrath of the Almighty was, at the reconciliation of the great Sovereign, restored again with all glory.

As for Antiochus, when he had carried away out of the temple a thousand and eight hundred talents, he departed in all haste unto Antioch, weening in his arrogancy to make the land navigable and the sea passable by foot, because his heart was lifted up. And moreover he left governors to afflict the race; at Jerusalem, Philip, by race a Phrygian, and in character more barbarous than him that set him there; and at Gerizim, Andronicus; and besides these, Menelaus, who worse than all the rest exalted himself against his fellow - citizens. And having a malicious mind toward the Jews whom he had made his citizens, he sent that lord of pollutions Apollonius with an army of two and twentythousand, commanding him to slay all those that were of full age, and to sell the women and the younger men. And he coming to Jerusalem, and playing the man of peace, waited till the holy day of the sabbath, and finding the Jews at rest from work, he commanded his men to parade in arms. And he put to the sword all them that came forth to the spectacle; and running into the city with the armed men he slew great multitudes. But Judas, who is also called Maccabaeus, with nine others or thereabout, withdrew himself, and with his company kept himself alive in the mountains after the manner of wild beasts; and they continued feeding on such poor herbs as grew there, that they might not be partakers of the threatened pollution.

CHAPTER VI

AND not long after this the king sent forth an old man of Athens to compel the Jews to depart from the laws of their fathers, and not to live after the laws of God; and also to pollute the sanctuary in Jerusalem, and to call it by the name of Jupiter Olympius, and to call the sanctuary in Gerizim by the name of Jupiter the Protector of strangers, even as they were that dwelt in the place. But sore and utterly grievous was the visitation of this evil. For the temple was filled with riot and revellings by the heathen, who dallied with harlots, and had to do with women within the sacred precincts, and moreover brought inside things that were not befitting; and the place of sacrifice was filled with those abominable things which had been prohibited by the laws. And a man could neither keep the sabbath, nor observe the feasts of the fathers, nor so much as confess himself to be a Jew. And on the day of the king's birth every month they were led along with bitter constraint to eat of the sacrifices; and when the feast of Bacchus came, they were compelled to go in procession in honour of Bacchus, wearing wreaths of ivy. And there went out a decree to the neighboring Greek cities, by the suggestion of Ptolemy, that they should observe the same conduct against the Jews, and should make them eat of the sacrifices; and that they should slay such as did not choose to go over to the Greek rites. So the present misery was for all to see: for two women were brought up for having circumcised their children; and these, when they had led them publicly round abut the city, with the babes hung from their breasts, they cast down headlong from the wall, And others, that had run together into the caves near by to keep the seventh day secretly, being betrayed to Philip were all burnt together, because they scrupled to defend themselves, from regard to the honour of that most solemn day.

I beseech therefore those that read this book, that they be not discouraged because of the calamities, but account that these punishments were not for the destruction, but for the chastening of our race. For indeed that those who act impiously be not let alone any long time, but straightway meet with retribution, is sign of great beneficence.

For in the case of the other nations the Sovereign Lord doth with long-suffering forbear, until that he punish them when they have attained unto the full measure of their sins; but not so judged he as touching us, that he may not take vengeance on us afterward, when we be come unto the height of our sins. Wherefore he never withdraweth his mercy from us; but though he chasteneth with calamity, yet doth he not forsake his own people. Howbeit let this that we have spoken suffice to put you in remembrance; but after these few words we must come to the narrative.

Eleazar, one of the principal scribes, a man already well stricken in years, and of a noble countenance, was compelled to open his mouth to eat swine's flesh. But he, welcoming death with renown rather than life with pollution, advanced of his own accord to the instrument of torture, but first spat forth the flesh, coming forward as men ought to come that are resolute to repel such things as not even for the natural love of life is it lawful to taste. But they that had the charge of that forbidden sacrificial feast took the man aside, for the acquaintance which of old times they had with him, and privately besought him to bring flesh of his own providing, such as was befitting for him to use, and to make as if he did eat of the flesh from the sacrifice, as had been commanded by the king; that by so doing he might be delivered from death, and for his ancient friendship with them might be treated kindly. But he, having formed a high resolve, and one that became his years, and the dignity of old age, and the gray hairs which he had reached with honour, and his excellent education from a child, or rather that became the holy laws of God's ordaining, declared his mind accordingly, bidding them quickly send him unto Hades. For it becometh not our years to dissemble, said he, that through this many of the young should suppose that Eleazar, the man of fourscore years and ten, had gone over unto an alien religion; and so they, by reason of my dissimulation, and for the sake of this brief and momentary life, should be led astray because of me, and thus I get to myself a pollution and a stain of mine old age. For even if for the present time I shall remove from me the punishment of men, yet shall I not escape the hands of the Almighty, either living or dead. Wherefore, by manfully parting with my life now, I will shew myself worthy of mine old age, and leave behind a noble ensample to the young to die willingly and nobly a glorious death for the reverend and holy laws. And when he had said these words, he went straightway to the instrument of torture. And when they changed the good will they bare him a little before into ill will, because these words of his were, as they thought, sheer madness, and when he was at the point to die with the stripes, he groaned aloud and said, To the Lord, that hath the holy knowledge, it is manifest that, whereas I might have been delivered from death, I endure sore pains in my body by being scourged; but in soul I gladly suffer these things for my fear of him. So this man also died after this manner, leaving his death for an ensample of nobleness and a memorial of virtue, not only to the young but also to the great body of his nation.

CHAPTER VII

AND it came to pass that seven brethren also with their mother were at the king's command taken and shamefully handled with scourges and cords, to compel them to taste of the abominable swine's flesh. But one of them made himself the spokesman and said, What wouldest thou ask and learn of us? for we are ready to die rather than transgress the laws of our fathers. And the king fell into a rage, and commanded to heat pans and caldrons; and when these forthwith were heated, he commanded to cut out the tongue of him that had been their spokesman, and to scalp him, and to cut off his extremities, the rest of his brethren and his mother looking on. And when he was utterly maimed, the king commanded to bring him to the fire, being yet alive, and to fry him in the pan. And as the vapour of the pan spread far, they and their mother also exhorted one another to die nobly, saying thus: The Lord God beholdeth, and in truth is intreated for us, as Moses declared in his song, which witnesseth against the people to their faces, saying, And he shall be intreated for his servants.

And when the first had died after this manner, they brought the second to the mocking; and they pulled off the skin of his head with the hair and asked him, Wilt thou eat, before thy body be punished in every limb ? But he answered in the language of his fathers and said to them, No. Wherefore he also underwent the next torture in succession, as the first had done. And when he was at the last gasp, he said, Thou, miscreant, dost release us out of this present life, but the King of the world shall raise up us, who have died for his laws, unto an eternal renewal of life.

And after him was the third made a mocking - stock. And when he was required, he quickly put out his tongue, and stretched forth his hands courageously, and nobly said, From heaven I possess these; and for his laws' sake I contemn these; and from him I hope to receive these back again: insomuch that the king himself and they that were with him were astonished at the young man's soul, for that he nothing regarded the pains.

And when he too was dead, they shamefully handled and tortured the fourth in like manner. And being come near unto death he said thus: It is good to die at the hands of men and look for the hopes which are given by God, that we shall be raised up again by him; for as for thee, thou shalt have no resurrection unto life.

And next after him they brought the fifth, and shamefully handled him. But he looked toward the king and said, Because thou hast authority among men, though thou art thyself corruptible, thou doest what thou wilt; yet think not that our race hath been forsaken of God; but hold thou on thy way, and behold his sovereign majesty, how it will torture thee and thy seed.

And after him they brought the sixth. And when he was at the point to die he said, Be not vainly deceived, for we suffer these things for our own doings, as sinning against our own God: marvellous things are come to pass; but think not thou that thou shalt be unpunished, having assayed to fight against God.

But above all was the mother marvellous and worthy of honourable memory; for when she looked on seven sons perishing within the space of one day, she bare the sight with a good courage for the hopes that she had set on the Lord. And she exhorted each one of them in the language of their fathers, filled with a noble temper and stirring up her womanish thought with manly passion, saying unto them, I know not how ye came into my womb, neither was it I that bestowed on you your spirit and your life, and it was not I that brought into order the first elements of each one of you. Therefore the Creator of the world, who fashioned the generation of man and devised the generation of all things, in mercy giveth back to you again both your spirit and your life, as ye now contemn your own selves for his laws' sake. But Antiochus, thinking himself to be despised, and suspecting the reproachful voice, whilst the youngest was yet alive did not only make his appeal to him by words, but also at the same time promised with oaths that he would enrich him and raise him to high estate, if he would turn from the customs of his fathers, and that he would take him for his Friend and intrust him with affairs. But when the young man would in no wise give heed, the king called unto him his mother, and exhorted her that she would counsel the lad to save himself. And when he had exhorted her with many words, she undertook to persuade her son. But bending toward him, laughing the cruel tyrant to scorn, she spake thus in the language of her fathers, My son, have pity upon me that carried thee nine months in my womb, and gave thee suck three years, and nourished and brought thee up unto this age, and sustained thee. I beseech thee, my child, to lift thine eyes unto the heaven and the earth, and to see all things that are therein, and thus to recognise that God made them not of things that were, and that the race of men in this wise cometh into being. Fear not this butcher, but, proving thyself worthy of thy brethren, accept thy death, that in the mercy of God I may receive thee again with thy brethren.

But before she had yet ended speaking, the young man said, Whom wait ye for ? I obey not the commandment of the king, but I hearken to the commandment of the law that was given to our fathers through Moses. But thou, that hast devised all manner of evil against the Hebrews, shalt in no wise escape the hands of God. For we are suffering because of our own sins; and if for rebuke and chastening our living Lord hath been angered a little while, yet shall he again be reconciled with his own servants. But thou, O unholy man and of all most vile, be not vainly lifted up in thy wild pride with uncertain hopes, raising thy hand against the heavenly children; for not yet hast thou escaped the judgement of the Almighty God that seeth all things. For these our brethren, having endured a short pain that bringeth everlasting life, have now died under God's covenant; but thou, through the judgement of God, shalt receive in just measure the penalties of thine arrogancy. But I, as my brethren, give up both body and soul for the laws of our fathers, calling upon God that he may speedily become gracious to the nation; and that thou amidst trials and plagues mayest confess that he alone is God; and that in me and my brethren thou mayest stay the wrath of the Almighty, which hath been justly brought upon our whole race. But the king, falling into a rage, handled him worse than all the rest, being exasperated at his mocking. So he also died pure from pollution, putting his whole trust in the Lord.

And last of all after her sons the mother died.

Let it then suffice to have said thus much concerning the enforcement of sacrificial feasts and the king's exceeding barbarities.

CHAPTER VIII

BUT Judas, who is also called Maccabaeus, and they that were with him, making their way privily into the villages, called unto them their kinsfolk; and taking unto them such as had continued in the Jews' religion, gathered together as many as six thousand. And they called upon the Lord, beseeching him to look upon the people that was oppressed by all; and to have compassion of the sanctuary also that had been profaned by the ungodly men; and to have pity on the city also that was suffering ruin and ready to be made even with the ground; and to hearken to the blood that cried unto him; and to remember also the lawless slaughter of the innocent infants, and the blasphemies that had been committed against his name, and to shew his hatred of wickedness. And when Maccabaeus had trained his men for service, the heathen at once found him irresistible, for that the wrath of the Lord was turned into pity. And coming unawares he set fire to cities and villages. And in winning back the most important positions, putting to flight no small number of the enemies, he specially took advantage of the nights for such assaults. And his courage was loudly talked of everywhere.

But when Philip saw the man gaining ground by little and little, and increasing more and more in his prosperity, he wrote unto Ptolemy, the governor of Coelesyria and Phoenicia, that he should support the king's cause. And Ptolemy quickly appointed Nicanor the son of Patroclus, one of the king's Chief Friends, and sent him, in command of no fewer than twenty thousand of all nations, to destroy the whole race of Judaea; and with him he joined Gorgias also, a captain and one that had experience in matters of war. And Nicanor undertook by the sale of the captive Jews to make up for the king the tribute of two thousand talents which he was to pay to the Romans. And immediately he sent unto the cities upon the sea coast, inviting them to buy Jewish slaves, promising to allow fourscore and ten slaves for a talent, not expecting thc judgement that was to follow upon him from the Almighty.

But tidings came to Judas concerning the inroad of Nicanor; and when he communicatcd to them that were with him the presence of the army, they that were cowardly and distrustful of the judgement of God ran away and left the country. And others sold all that was left over to them, and withal besought the Lord to deliver them that had been sold as slaves by the impious Nicanor or ever he met them; and this, if not for their own sakes, yet for the covenants made with their fathers, and be cause he had called them by his reverend and glorious name. And Maccabaeus gathered his men together, six thousand in number, and exhorted them not to be stricken with dismay at the enemy, nor to fear the great multitude of the heathen who came wrongfully against them; but to contend nobly, setting before their eyes the outrage that had been lawlessly perpetrated upon the holy place, and the shameful handling of the city that had been turned to mockery, and further the overthrow of the mode of life received from their ancestors. For they, said he, trust to arms, and withal to deeds of daring; but we trust on the Almighty God, since he is able at a beck to cast down them that are coming against us, and even the whole world. And moreover he recounted unto them the help given from time to time in the days of their ancestors, both the help given in the days of Sennacherib, how that a hundred fourscore and five thousand perished, and the help given in the land of Babylon even the battle that was fought against the Gauls, how that they came to the engagement eight thousand in all, with four thousand Macedonians, and how that, the Macedonians being hard pressed, the six thousand destroyed the hundred and twenty thousand, because of the succour which they had from heaven, and took great booty. And when he had with these words made them of good courage, and ready to die for the laws and their country, he divided his army into four parts; appointing his brethren to be with himself leaders of the several bands, to wit, Simon and Joseph and Jonathan, giving each the command of fifteen hundred men, and moreover Eleazar also: then, having read aloud the sacred book, and having given as watchword, THE HELP OF GOD, leading the first band himself; he joined battle with Nicanor. And, since the Almighty fought on their side they slew of the enemy above nine thousand, and wounded and disabled the more part of Nicanor's army, and compelled all to flee; and they took the money of those that had come there to buy them. And after they had pursued them for some distance, they returned, being constrained by the time of the day; for it was the day before the sabbath, and for this cause they made no effort to chase them far. And when they had gathered the arms of the enemy together, and had stripped off their spoils, they occupied themselves about the sabbath, blessing and thanking the Lord exceedingly, who had saved them unto this day, for that he had caused a beginning of mercy to distil upon them. And after the sabbath, when they had given of the spoils to the maimed, and to the widows and orphans, the residue they distributed among themselves and their children. And when they had accomplished these things, and had made a common supplication, they besought the merciful Lord to be wholly reconciled with his servants.

And having had an encounter with the forces of Timotheus and Bacchides, they killed above twenty thousand of them, and made themselves masters of strongholds exceeding high, and divided very much plunder, giving the maimed and orphans and widows, and moreover the aged also, an equal share with themselves. And when they had gathered the arms of the enemy together, they stored them all up carefully in the most important positions, and the residue of the spoils they carried to Jerusalem. And they killed the phylarch of Timotheus's forces, a most unholy man, and one who had done the Jews much hurt. And as they kept the feast of victory in the city of their fathers, they burned those that had set the sacred gates on fire, and among them Callisthenes, who had fled into an outhouse; and so they received the meet reward of their impiety.

And the thrice-accursed Nicanor, who had brought the thousand merchants to buy the Jews for slaves, being through the help of the Lord humbled by them who in his eyes were held to be of least account, put off his glorious apparel, and passing through the midland, shunning all company like a fugitive slave, arrived at Antioch, having, as he thought, had the greatest possible good fortune, though his host was destroyed. And he that had taken upon him to make tribute sure for the Romans by the captivity of the men of Jerusalem published abroad that the Jews had One who fought for them, and that because this was so the Jews were invulnerable, because they followed the laws ordained by him.

CHAPTER IX

NOW about that time it befell that Antiochus had returned in disorder from the region of Persia. For he had entered into the city called Persepolis, and he assayed to rob a temple and to hold down the city. Whereupon there was an onset of the multitudes, and Antiochus and his men turned to make defense with arms; and it came to pass that Antiochus was put to flight by the people of the country and broke up his camp with disgrace. And while he was at Ecbatana, news was brought him what had happened unto Nicanor and the forces of Timotheus. And being lifted up by his passion he thought to make the Jews suffer even for the evil-doing of those that had put him to rout. Wherefore, the judgement from heaven even now accompanying him, he gave order to his charioteer to drive without ceasing and dispatch the journey; for thus he arrogantly spake: I will make Jerusalem a common graveyard of Jews, when I come there. But the All-seeing Lord, the God of Israel, smote him with a fatal and invisible stroke; and as soon as he had ceased speaking this word, an incurable pain of the bowels seized him, and bitter torments of the inner parts; and that most justly, for he had tormented other men's bowels with many and strange sufferings. But he in no wise ceased from his rude insolence; nay, still more was he filled with arrogance, breathing fire in his passion against the Jews, and commanding to haste the journey. But it came to pass moreover that he fell from his chariot as it rushed along, and having a grievous fall was racked in all the members of his body. And he that but now supposed himself to have the waves of the sea at his bidding; so vainglorious was he beyond the condition of a man, and that thought to weigh the heights of the mountains in a balance, was now brought to the ground and carried in a litter, shewing unto all that the power was manifestly God's; so that out of the body of the impious man worms swarmed, and while he was still living in anguish and pains, his flesh fell off, and by reason of the stench all the army turned with loathing from his corruption. And the man that a little afore supposed himself to touch the stars of heaven, no one could endure to carry for his intolerable stench. Hereupon therefore he began in great part to cease from his arrogancy, being broken 'in spirit, and to come to knowledge under the scourge of God, his pains increasing every moment. And when he himself could not abide his own smell, he said these words: It is right to be subject unto God, and that one who is mortal should not be minded arrogantly. And the vile man vowed unto the Sovereign Lord, who now no more would have pity upon him, saying on this wise: that the holy city, to the which he was going in haste, to lay it even with the ground and to make it a common graveyard, he would declare free; and as touching the Jews, whom he had decided not even to count worthy of burial, but to cast them out to the beasts with their infants, for the birds to devour, he would make them all equal to citizens of Athens, and the holy sanctuary, which before he had spoiled, he would adorn with goodliest offerings, and would restore all the sacred vessels many times multiplied, and out of his own revenues would defray the charges that were required for the sacrifices; and, beside all this, that he would become a Jew, and would visit every inhabited place, publishing abroad the might of God. But when his sufferings did in no wise cease, for the judgement of God had come upon him in righteousness, having given up all hope of himself, he wrote unto the Jews the letter written below, having the nature of a supplication, to this effect:

To the worthy Jews, his fellow-citizens, Antiochus, king and general, wisheth much joy and health and prosperity. May ye and your children fare well; and your affairs shall be to your mind. Having my hope in heaven, I remembered with affection your honour and good will toward me. Returning out of thc region of Persia, and being taken with a noisome sickness, I deemcd it necessary to take thought for the common safety of all, not despairing of myself, but having great hope to escape from the sickness. But considering that my father also, at what time he led an army into the upper country, appointed his successor, to the end that, if anything fell out contrary to expectation, or if any unwelcome tidings were brought, they that remained in the country, knowing to whom the state had been left, might not be troubled; and, beside all this, observing how that the princes that are borderers and neighbours unto my kingdom watch opportunities, and look for the future event, I have appointed my son Antiochus to be king, whom I often committed and commended to most of you, when I was hastening unto the upper provinces; and I have written to him what is written below. I exhort you therefore and beseech you, having in your remembrance the benefits done to you in common and severally, to preserve each of you your present good will toward me and my son. For I am persuaded that he in gentleness and kindness will follow my purpose and treat you with indulgence.

So the murderer and blasphemer, having endured the sorest sufferings, even as he had dealt with other men, ended his life among the mountains by a most piteous fate in a strange land. And Philip his foster-brother conveyed the body home; and then, fearing the son of Antiochus, he betook himself to Ptolemy Philometor in Egypt.

CHAPTER X

AND Maccabaeus and they that were with him, the Lord leading them on, recovered the temple and the city; and they pulled down the altars that had been built in the market-place by the aliens, and also the walls of sacred inclosures. And having cleansed the sanctuary they made another altar of sacrifice; and striking stones and taking fire out of them, they offered sacrifices, after they had ceased for two years, and burned incense, and lighted lamps, and set forth the shewbread. And when they had done these things, they fell prostrate and besought the Lord that they might fall no more into such evils; but that, if ever they should sin, they might be chastened by him with forbearance, and not be delivered unto blaspheming and barbarous heathen. Now on the same day that the sanctuary was profaned by aliens, upon that very day did it come to pass that the cleansing of the sanctuary was made, even on the five and twentieth day of the same month, which is Chislev. And they kept eight days with gladness in the manner of the feast of tabernacles, remembering how that not long afore, during the feast of tabernacles, they were wandering in thc mountains and in the caves after the manner of wild beasts. Wherefore bearing wands wreathed with leaves, and fair boughs, and palms also, they offered up hymns of thanksgiving to him that had prosperously brought to pass the cleansing of his own place. They ordained also with a common statute and decree, for all the nation of the Jews, that they should keep these days every year.

And such was the end of Antiochus, who was called Epiphanes. But now will we declare what came to pass under Antiochus named Eupator, who proved himself a true son of that ungodly man, and will gather up briefly the successive evils of the wars. For this man, when he succeeded to the kingdom, appointed one Lysias to be chancellor, and supreme governor of Coelesyria and Phoenicia. For Ptolemy that was called Macron, setting an example of observing justice toward the Jews because of the wrong that had been unto them, endeavoured to conduct his dealings with them on peaceful terms. Whereupon being accused by the king's Friends before Eupator, and hearing himself called traitor at every turn, because he had abandoned Cyprus which Philometor had intrusted to him, and had withdrawn himself unto Antiochus called Epiphanes, and failing to uphold the honour of his office, he took poison and made away with himself.

But Gorgias, when he was made governor of the district, maintained a force of mercenaries, and at every turn kept up war with the Jews. And together with him the Idumaenms also, being masters of important strongholds, harassed the Jews; and receiving unto them those that had taken refuge there from Jerusalem, they assayed to keep up war. But Maccabeaus and his men, having made solemn supplication and besought God to fight on their side, rushed upon the strongholds of the Idumaeans; and assaulting them vigorously they made themselves master of the positions, and kept off all that fought upon the wall, and slew those that fell in their way, and killed no fewer than twenty thousand. And because no less than nine thousand were fled into two towers exceeding strong and having all things needed for a siege, Maccabeaus, having left Simon and Joseph, and Zacchaeus beside and them that were with him, a force sufficient to besiege them, departed himself unto places where he was most needed. But Simon and they that were with him, yielding to covetousness, were bribed by certain of those that were in the towers, and receiving seventy thousand drachmas let some of them slip away. But when word was brought to Maccabeaus of what was done, he gathered the leaders of the people together, and accused those men of having sold their brethren for money, by setting their enemies free to fight against them. So he slew these men for having turned traitors, and forthwith took possession of the two towers. And prospering with his arms in all things he took in hand, he destroyed in the two strongholds more than twenty thousand.

Now Timotheus, who had been before defeated by the Jews, having gathered together foreign forces in great multitudes, and having collected the horsemen which belonged to Asia, not a few, came as though he would take Judea by force of arms. But as he draw near, Maccabaeus and his men sprinkled earth upon their heads and girded their loins with sackcloth, in supplication to God, and falling down upon the step in front of the after, besought him to become gracious to them, and be an enemy to their enemies and an adversary to their adversaries, as the law declareth. And rising from their prayer they took up their arms, and advanced some distance from the city; and when they had come near to their enemies they halted. And when the dawn was now spreading, the two armies joined battle; the one part having this, beside their virtue, for a pledge of success and victory, that they had fled unto the Lord for refuge, the others making their passion their leader in the strife. But when the battle waxed strong, there appeared out of heaven unto their adversaries five men on horses with bridles of gold, in splendid array; and two of them, leading on the Jews and taking Maccabaeus in the midst of them, and covering him with their own armour, guarded him from wounds, while on the adversaries they shot forth arrows and thunderbolts; by reason whereof they were blinded and thrown into confusion, and were cut to pieces, filled with bewilderment. And there were slain twenty thousand and five hundred, beside six hundred horsemen.

But Timotheus himself fled into a stronghold called Gazara, a fortress of exceeding strength, Chaereas being in command there. But Maccabaeus and his men were glad and laid siege to the fortress four and twenty days. And they that were within, trusting to the strength of the place, blasphemed exceedingly, and hurled forth impious words. But at dawn of the five and twentieth day certain young men of the company of Maccabaeus, inflamed with passion because of the blasphemies, assaulted the wall with masculine force and with furious passion, and cut down whosoever came in their way. And others climbing up in like manner, while the besieged were distracted with them that had made their way within, set fire to the towers, and kindling fires burned the blasphemers alive; while others broke open the gates, and, having given entrance to the rest of the band, occupied the city. And they slew Timotheus, who was hidden in a cistern, and his brother Chaereas, and Apollophanes. And when they had accomplished these things, they blessed the Lord with hymns and thanksgivings, him who doeth great benefits unto Israel, and giveth them the victory.

CHAPTER XI

NOW after a very little time Lysias, the king's guardian and kinsman and chancellor, being sore displeased for the things that had come to pass, collected about fourscore thousand footmen and all his horsemen and came against the Jews, thinking to make the city a place for Greeks to dwell in, and to levy tribute on the temple, as on the other sacred places of the nations, and to put up the high priesthood to sale every year; holding in no account the might of God, but puffed up with his ten thousands of footmen, and his thousands of horsemen, and his fourscore elephants. And coming into Judaea and drawing near to Bethsuron, which was a strong place and distant from Jerusalem about five leagues, he pressed it hard. But when Maccabaeus and his men learned that he was besieging the strongholds, they and all the people with lamentations and tears made supplication unto the Lord to send a good angel to save Israel. And Maccabaeus himself took up arms first, and exhorted the others to jeopard themselves together with him and succour their brethren; and they sallied forth with him right willingly. And as they were there, close to Jerusalem, there appeared at their head one on horseback in white apparel, brandishing weapons of gold. And they all together praised the merciful God, and were yet more strengthened in heart: being ready to assail not men only but the wildest beasts, and walls of iron, they advanced in array, having him that is in heaven to fight on their side, for the Lord had mercy on them. And hurling themselves like lions upon the enemy, they slew of them eleven thousand footmen and sixteen hundred horsemen, and forced all the rest to flee. But the more part of them escaped wounded and naked; and Lysias also himself escaped by shameful flight. But as he was a man not void of understanding, weighing with himself the defeat which had befallen him, and considering that the Hebrews could not be overcome, because the Almighty God fought on their side, he sent again unto them, and persuaded them to come to terms on condition that all their rights were acknowledged, and promised that he would also persuade the king to become their friend. And Maccabaeus gave consent upon all the conditions which Lysias proposed to him, being careful of the common good; for whatsoever requests Maccabaeus delivered in writing unto Lysias concerning the Jews the king allowed. For the letters written unto the Jews were from Lysias to this effect:

Lysias unto the people of the Jews, greeting. John and Absalom, who were sent from you, having delivered the petition written below, made request concerning the things signified therein. What thing soever therefore had need to be brought before the king I declared to him, and what things were possible he allowed. If then ye will preserve your good will toward the state, henceforward also will I endeavour to contribute to your good. And on this behalf I have given order in detail, both to these men and to those that are sent from me, to confer with you. Fare ye well. Written in the hundred forty and eighth year, on the four and twentieth day of the month Dioscorinthius.

And the king's letter was in these words:

King Antiochus unto his brother Lysias, greeting. Seeing that our father passed unto the gods having the wish that the subjects of his kingdom should be undisturbed and give themselves to the care of their own affairs, we, having heard that the Jews do not consent to our father's purpose to turn them unto the customs of the Greeks, but choose rather their own manner of living, and make request that the customs of their law be allowed unto them, - choosing therefore that this nation also should be free from disturbance, we determine that their temple be restored to them, and that they live according to the customs that were in the days of their ancestors. Thou wilt therefore do well to send messengers unto them and give them the right hand of friendship, that they, knowing our mind, may be of good heart, and gladly occupy themselves with the conduct of their own affairs.

And unto the nation the king's letter was after this manner:

King Antiochus to the senate of the Jews and to the other Jews, greetings. If ye fare well, we have our desire: we ourselves also are in good health. Menelaus informed us that your desire was to return home and follow your own business. They therefore that depart home up to the thirtieth day of Xanthicus shall have our friendship, with full permission that the Jews use their own proper meats and observe their own laws, even as heretofore; and none of them shall be in any way molested for the things that have been ignorantly done. Moreover I have sent Menelaus also, that he may encourage you. Fare ye well. Written in the hundred forty and eighth year, on the fifteenth day of Xanthicus.

And the Romans also sent unto them a letter in these words:

Quintus Memmius and Titus Manius, ambassadors of the Romans, unto the people of the Jews, greeting. In regard to the things which Lysias the king's kinsman granted you, we also give consent. But as for the things which he judged should be referred to the king, send one forthwith, after ye have advised thereof, that we may publish such decrees as befit your case; for we are on our way to Antioch. Wherefore send some with speed, that we also may learn what is your mind. Farewell. Written in the hundred forty and eighth year on the fifteenth day of Xanthicus.

CHAPTER XII

SO when these covenants had been made, Lysias departed unto the king, and the Jews went about their husbandry.

But certain of the governors of districts, Timotheus and Apollonius the son of Gennaeus, and Hieronymus also and Demophon, and beside them Nicanor the governor of Cyprus, would not suffer them to enjoy tranquillity and live in peace. And men of Joppa perpetrated this great impiety: they invited the Jews that dwelt among them to go with their wives and children into the boats which they had provided, as though they had no ill will towards them; and when the Jews, relying on the common decree of the city, accepted the invitation, as men desiring to live in peace and suspecting nothing, they took them out to sea and drowned them, in number not less than two hundred. But when Judas heard of the cruelty done unto his fellow-countrymen, giving command to the men that were with him and calling upon God the righteous Judge, he came against the murderers of his brethren, and set the haven on fire by night, and burned the boats, and put to the sword those that had fled thither. But when the town was closed against him, he withdrew, intending to come again to root out the whole community of the men of Joppa. But learning that the men of Jamnia were minded to do in like manner unto the Jews that sojourncd among them, he fell upon the Jamnites also by night, and set fire to the haven together with the fleet, so that the glare of the light was seen at Jerusalem, two hundred and forty furlongs distant.

Now when they had drawn off nine furlongs from thence, as they marched against Timotheus, a host of Arabians attacked him, no fewer than five thousand footmen and five hundred horsemen. And when a sore battle had been fought, and Judas and his company by the help of God had good success, the nomads being overcome besought Judas to grant them friendship, promising to give him cattle, and to help his people in all other ways. So Judas, thinking that they would indeed be profitable in many things, agreed to live in peace with them; and receiving pledges of friendship they departed to their tents. And he also fell upon a certain city Gephyrun, strong and fenced about with walls, and inhabited by a mixed multitude of divers nations; and it was named Caspin. But they that were within, trusting to the strength of the walls and to their store of provisions, behaved themselves rudely toward Judas and them that were with him, railing, and furthermore blaspheming and speaking impious words. But

Judas and his company, calling upon the great Sovereign of the world, who without rams and cunning engines of war hurled down Jericho in the times of Joshua, rushed wildly against the wall; and having taken the city by the will of God, they made unspeakable slaughter, insomuch that the adjoining lake, which was two furlongs broad, appeared to be filled with the deluge of blood.

And when they had drawn off seven hundred and fifty furlongs from thence, they made their way to Charax, unto the Jews that are called Tubieni. And Timotheus they found not in occupation of that district, for he had then departed from the district without accomplishing anything, but had left behind a garrison, and that a very strong one, in a certain post. But Dositheus and Sosipater, who were of Maccabaeus's captains, sallied forth and destroyed those that had been left by Timotheus in the stronghold, above ten thousand men. And Maccabaeus, ranging his own army by bands, set these two over the bands, and marched in haste against Timotheus, who had with him a hundred and twenty thousand footmen and two thousand and five hundred horsemen. But when Timotheus heard of the inroad of Judas, he at once sent away the women and the children and also the baggage into the fortress called Carnion; for the place was hard to besiege and difficult of access by reason of the narrowness of the approaches on all sides. But when the band of Judas, who led the van, appeared in sight, and when terror came upon the enemy and fear, because the manifestation of him who beholdeth all things came upon them, they fled amain, carried this way and that, so that they were often hurt of their own men, and pierced with the points of their swords. And Judas continued the pursuit the more hotly, putting the wicked wretches to the sword, and he destroyed as many as thirty thousand men. But Timotheus himself, falling in with the company of Dositheus and Sosipater, besought them with much crafty guile to let him go with his life, because he had in his power the parents of many of them and the brethren of some: otherwise, said he, little regard will be shown to these. So when he had with many words confirmed the agreement to restore them without hurt, they let him go that they might save their brethren.

And Judas, marching against Carnion and the temple of Atergatis, slew five and twenty thousand persons. And after he had put these to flight and destroyed them, he marched against Ephron also, a strong city, wherein were multitudes of people of all nations; and stalwart young men placed on the walls made a vigorous defence; and there were great stores of engines and darts there. But calling upon the Sovereign who with might breaketh in pieces the strength of the enemy, they got the city into their hands, and slew as many as twenty and five thousand of them that were within. And setting out from thence they marched in haste against Scythopolis, which is distant from Jerusalem six hundred furlongs. But when they Jews that were settled there testified of the good will that the Scythopolitans had shown toward them, and of their kindly bearing toward them in the times of their misfortune, they gave thanks, and further exhorted them to remain well affected toward the race for the future; and they went up to Jerusalem, the feast of weeks being close at hand.

But after the feast called Pentecost they marched in haste against Gorgias the governor of Idumaea: and he came out with three thousand footmen and four hundred horsemen. And when they had set themselves in array, it came to pass that a few of the Jews fell. And a certain Dositheus, one of Bacenor's company, who was on horseback and a strong man, pressed hard on Gorgias, and taking hold of his cloke drew him along by main force; and while he was minded to take the accursed man alive, one of the Thracian horsemen bore down upon him and disabled his shoulder, and so Gorgias escaped unto Marisa. And when they that were with Esdris had been fighting long and were wearied out, Judas called upon the Lord to shew himself, fighting on their side and leading the van of the battle; and then in the language of his fathers he raised the battle-cry joined with hymns, and rushing unawares upon the troops of Gorgias put them to flight.

And Judas gathering his army came unto thc city of Adullam; and as the seventh day was coming on, they purified themselves according to the custom, and kept the sabbath there. And on the day following, at which time it had become necessary, Judas and his company camc to take up the bodies of them that had fallen, and in company with their kinsmen to bring them back unto the sepulchres of their fathers. But under the garments of each one of the dead they found consecrated tokens of the idols of Jamnia, which the law forbids the Jews to have aught to do with; and it became clear to all that it was for this cause that they had fallen. All therefore, blessing the works of the Lord, the righteous Judge, who maketh manifest the things that are hid, betook themselves unto supplication, beseeching that the sin committed might be wholly blotted out. And the noble Judas exhorted the multitude to keep themselves from sin, forsomuch as they had seen before their eyes what things had come to pass because of the sin of them that had fallen. And when he had made a collection man by man to the sum of two thousand drachmas of silver, he sent unto Jerusalem to offer a sacrifice for sin, doing therein right well and honourably, in that he took thought for a resurrection. For if he were not expecting that they that had fallen would rise again, it were superfluous and idle to pray for the dead. (And if he did it looking unto an honourable memorial of gratitude laid up for them that die in godliness, holy and godly was the thought.) Wherefore he made the propitiation for them that had died, that they might be released from their sin.

CHAPTER XIII

IN the hundred forty and ninth year tidings were brought to Judas and his company that Antiochus Eupator was coming with great multitudes against Judaea, and with him Lysias his guardian and chancellor, each having a Greek force, a hundred and ten thousand footmen, and five thousand and three hundred horsemen, and two and twenty elephants, and three hundred chariots armed with scythes.

And Menelaus also joined himself with them, and with great dissimulation encouraged Antiochus, not for the saving of his country, but because he thought that he would be set over the government. But the King of kings stirred up the passion of Antiochus against the wicked wretch; and when Lysias informed him that this man was the cause of all the evils, the king commanded to bring him unto Beroea, and to put him to death after the manner of that place. Now there is in that place a tower of fifty cubits high, full of ashes, and it had all round it a gallery descending sheer on every side into the ashes. Here him that is guilty of sacrilege, or hath attained a preeminence in any other evil deeds, they all push forward into destruction. By such a fate it befell the breaker of the law, Menelaus, to die, without obtaining so much as a grave in the earth, and that right justly; for inasmuch as he had perpetrated many sins against the altar, whose fire and whose ashes were holy, in ashes did he receive his death.

Now the king, infuriated in spirit, was coming with intent to inflict on the Jews the very worst of the sufferings that had befallen them in his father's time. But when

Judas heard of these things, he gave charge to the multitude to call upon the Lord day and night, beseeching him, if ever at any other time, so now to succour them that were at the point to be deprived of the law and their country and the holy temple, and not to suffer the people that had been but now a little while revived to fall into the hands of those profane heathen. So when they had all done the same thing together, beseeching the merciful Lord with weeping and fastings and prostration for three days without ceasing, Judas exhorted them and commanded they should join him for service. And having gone apart with the elders he resolved that, before the king's army should enter into Judaea and make themselves masters of the city, they should go forth and try the matter in fight by the help of God. And committing the decision to the Lord of the world, and exhorting them that were with him to contend nobly even unto death for laws, temple, city, country, commonwealth, he pitched his camp by Modin. And having given out to his men the watchword, VICTORY IS GOD'S, with a chosen body of the bravest young men he fell upon the camp by night and penetrated to the king's tent, and slew of the army as many as two thousand men, and brought down the chiefest elephant with him that was in the tower upon him. And at last they filled the army with terror and alarm, and departed with good success. And this had been accomplished when the day was but now dawning, because of the Lord's protection that gave Judas help.

But the king, having had a taste of the exceeding boldness of the Jews, made attempts by stratagem upon their positions, and upon a strong fortress of the Jews at Bethsura; he advanced, was turned back, failed, was defeated. And Judas conveyed such things as were necessary unto them that were within. But Rhodocus, from the Jewish ranks, made known to the enemy the secrets of his countrymen. He was sought out, and taken, and shut up in prison. The king treated with them in Bethsura the second time, gave his hand, took theirs, departed, attacked the forces of Judas, was put to the worse, heard that Philip who had been left as chancellor in Antioch had become reckless, was confounded, made to the Jews an overture of peace, submitted himself and sware to acknowledge all their rights, came to terms with them and offered sacrifice, honoured the sanctuary and the place, shewed kindness and graciously received Maccabaeus, lelt Hegemonides governor from Ptolemais even unto the Gerrenians, came to Ptolemais. The men of Ptolemais were displeased at the treaty, for they had exceeding great indignation against the Jews: they desired to annul the articles of the agreement. Lysias came forward to speak, made the best defence that was possible, persuaded, pacified, made them well affected, departed unto Antioch. This was the issue of the inroad and departure of the king.

CHAPTER XIV

NOW aftcr a space of three years tidings were brought to Judas and his company that Demetrius the son of Seleucus, having sailed into the haven of Tripolis with a mighty host and a fleet, had gotten possession of the country, having madc away with Antiochus and Lysias his guardian.

But one Alcimus, who had formerly been high priest, and had wilfully pollutcd himself in the times when there was no mingling with the Gentiles, considering that there was no deliverance for him in any way, nor any more access unto the holy altar, came to king Demetrius in about the hundred and one and fiftieth year, presenting to him a chaplet of gold and a palm, and beside these some of the festal olive boughs of the temple. And for that day he held his peace; but having gotten opportunity to further his own madness, being called by Demetrius into a meeting of his council, and asked how the Jews stood affected and what they purposed, he answered thereunto, Those of the Jews that be called Hasidaeans, whose leader is Judas Maccabaeus, keep up war, and are seditious, not suffering the kingdom to find tranquillity. Wherefore, having laid aside mine ancestral glory, I mean the high priesthood, I am now come hither; first for the unfeigned care I have for the things that concern the king, and secondly because I have regard also to mine own fellow-citizens: for, through the unadvised dealing of those of whom I spake before, our whole race is in no small misfortune. But do thou, O king, having informed thyself of these things severally, take thought both for our country and for our race, which is surrounded by foes, according to the gracious kindness with which thou receivest all. For as long as Judas remaineth alive, it is impossiblc that the state should find peace. And when he had spokcn such words as these, at once the rest of the king's Friends having ill will against Judas, inflamed Demetrius yet more. And forthwith appointing Nicanor, who had been master of the elephants, and making him governor of Judaea, he sent him forth, giving him written instructions to make away with Judas himself and to scatter them that were with him, and to set up Alcimus as high priest of the great temple. And those in Judaea that had before driven Judas into exile thronged to Nicanor in flocks, supposing that the misfortunes and calamities of the Jews would be successes to themselves.

But when the Jews heard of Nicanor's inroad and the assault of the heathen, they sprinkled earth upon their heads and made solemn supplication to him who had established his own people for evermore, and who alway, making manifest his presence, upholdeth them that are his own portion. And when the leader had given his commands, he straightway setteth out from thence, and joineth battle with them at a village called Lessau. But Simon, the brother of Judas, had encountered Nicanor, yet not till late, having rcceived a check by reason of the sudden consternation caused by his adversaries.

Nevertheless Nicanor, hearing of the manliness of them that were with Judas, and their courage in fighting for their country, shrank from bringing the matter to the decision of the sword. Wherefore he sent Posidonius and Theodotus and Mattathias to give and receive pledges of friendship. So when these proposals had been long considered, and the leader had made the troops acquainted therewith, and it appeared that they were all of like mind, they consented to the covenants. And they appointed a day on which to meet together by themselves. And a litter was borne forward from each army; they set chairs of state; Judas stationed armed men ready in convenient places, lest haply there should suddenly be treachery on the part of thc enemy; they held such conference as was meet. Nicanor tarried in Jerusalem, and did nothing to cause disturbance, but dismissed the flocks of people that had gathered together. And he kept Judas always in his presence; he had gained a hearty affection for the man; he urged him to marry and beget children; he married, settled quietly, took part in common life.

But Alcimus, perceiving the good will that was betwixt them, and having got possession of the covenants that had been made, came unto Demetrius and told him that Nicanor was ill affected toward the state, for he had appointed that conspirator against his kingdom, Judas, to be his successor. And the king, falling into a rage, and being exasperated by the calumnies of that most wicked man, wrote to Nicanor, signifying that he was displeased at the covenants, and commanding him to send Maccabaeus prisoner unto Antioch in all haste. And when this message came to Nicanor, he was confounded, and was sore troubled, at the thought of annulling the articles that had been agreed upon, the man having done no wrong; but because there was no dealing against the king, he watched his time to execute this purpose by stratagem. But Maccabaeus, when he perceived that Nicanor was behaving more harshly in his dealings with him, and that he had become ruder in his customary bearing, understanding that this harshness came not of good, gathered together not a few of his men, and concealed himself from Nicanor.

But the other, when he became aware that he had been bravely defeated by the stratagem of Judas, came to the great and holy temple, while the priests were offering the usual sacrifices, and commanded them to deliver up the man. And when they declared with oaths that they had no knowledge where the man was whom he sought, he stretched forth his right hand toward the sanctuary, and sware this oath: If ye will not deliver up to me Judas as a prisoner, I will lay this temple of God even with the ground, and will break down the altar, and I will erect here a temple unto Bacchus for all to see. And having said this he departed. But the priests, stretching forth their hands toward heaven, called upon him that ever fighteth for our nation, in these words: Thou, O Lord of the universe, who in thyself hast need of nothing, wast well pleased that a sanctuary of thy habitation should be set among us; so now, O holy Lord of all hallowing, keep undefiled for ever this house that hath been lately cleansed.

Now information was given to Nicanor against one Razis, an elder of Jerusalem, as being a lover of his countrymen and a man of very good report, and one called Father of the Jews for his good will toward them. For in the former times when there was no mingling with the Gentiles he had been accused of cleaving to the Jews' religion, and had jeoparded body and life with all earnestness for the religion of the Jews. And Nicanor, wishing to make evident the ill will that he bare unto the Jews. sent above five hundred soldiers to take him; for he thought by taking him to inflict a calamity upon them. But when the troops were on the point of taking the tower, and were forcing the doors of the court, and bade bring fire and burn the doors, he being surrounded on every side fell upon his sword, choosing rather to die nobly than to fall into the hands of the wicked wretches, and suffer outrage unworthy of his own nobleness: but since he missed his stroke through the excitement of the struggle, and the crowds were now rushing within the door, he ran bravely up to the wall and cast himself down manfully among the crowds. But as they quickly gave back, a space was made, and he fell on the middle of his side. And having yet breath within him, and being inflamed with passion, he rose up, and though his blood gushed out in streams and his wounds were grievous, he ran through the crowds, and standing upon a steep rock, when as his blood was now well nigh spent, he drew forth his bowels through the wound, and taking them in both hands he shook them at the crowds; and calling upon him who is Lord of the life and the spirit to restore him these again, he thus died.

CHAPTER XV

BUT Nicanor, bearing that Judas and his company were in the region of Samria, resolved to set upon them with all security on the day of rest. And when the Jews that were compelled to follow him said, 0 destroy not so savagely and barbarously, but give due glory to the day which he that beholdeth all things hath honoured and hallowed above other days; then the thrice-accursed wretch asked if there were a Sovereign in heaven that had commanded to keep the sabbath day. And when they declared, There is the

Sovereign in heaven, who bade us observe the seventh day; then saith the other, I also am a sovereign upon the earth, who now command to take up arms and execute the king's business. Nevertheless he prevailed not to execute his cruel purpose.

And Nicanor; bearing himself haughtily in all vain-gloriousness, had determined to set up a monument of complete victory-over Judas and all them that were with him: but Maccabaeus still trusted unceasingly, with all hope that he should obtain help from the Lord. And he exhorted his company not to be fearful at the inroad of the heathen, but, keeping in mind the help which of old they had oft-times received from heaven, so now also to look for the victory which would come unto them from the Almighty; and comforting them out of the law and the prophets, and withal putting them in mind of the conflicts that they had maintained, he made them more eager for the battle. And when he had roused their spirit, he gave them his commands, at the same time pointing out the perfidiousness of the heathen and their breach of their oaths. And arming each one of them, not so much with the sure defence of shields and spears as with the encouragement that lieth in good words, and moreover relating to them a dream worthy to be believcd, he made them all exceeding glad. And the vision of that dream was this: He saw Onias, him that was high priest, a noble and good man, reverend in bearing, yet gentle in manner and well-spoken, and exercised from a child in all points of virtue, with outstretched hands invoking blessings on the whole body of the Jews: thereupon he saw a man appear, of venerable age and exceeding glory, and wonderful and most majestic was the dignity around him: and Onias answered and said, This is the lover of the brethren, he who prayeth much for the people and the holy city, Jeremiah the prophet of God: and Jeremiah stretching forth his right hand delivered to Judas a sword of gold, and in giving it addressed him thus, Take the holy sword, a gift from God, wherewith thou shalt smite down the adversaries.

And being encouraged by the words of Judas, which were of a lofty strain, and able to incite unto virtue and to stir the souls of the young unto manly courage, they determined not to carry on a campaign, but nobly to bear down upon the enemy, and fighting hand to hand with all courage bring the matter to an issue, because the city and the sanctuary and the temple were in danger. For their fear for wives and children, and furthermore for brethren and kinsfolk, was in less account with them; but greatest and first was their fear for the consecrated sanctuary. And they also that were shut up in the city were in no light distress, being troubled because of the encounter in the open ground.

And when all were now waiting for the decision of the issue, and the enemy had already joined battle, and the army had been set in array, and the elephants brought back to a convenient post and the horsemen drawn up on the flank, Maccabaeus, perceiving the presence of the troops, and the various arms with which they were equipped, and the savageness of the elephants, holding up his hands unto heaven called upon the Lord that worketh wonders, recognising that success cometh not by arms, but that, according as the Lord shall judge, he gaineth the victory for them that are worthy. And calling upon God he said after this manner: Thou, O Sovereign Lord, didst send thine angel in the time of Hezekiah king of Judaea, and he slew of the host of Sennacherib as many as a hundred fourscore and five thousand; so now also, O Sovereign of the heavens, send a good angel before us to bring terror and trembling: through the greatness of thine arm let them be stricken with dismay that with blasphemy are come hither against thy holy people. And as he ended with these words, Nicanor and his company advanced with trumpets and paeans; but Judas and his company joined battle with the enemy with invocation and prayers. And contending with their hands, and praying unto God with their hearts, they slew no less than thirty and five thousand men, being made exceeding glad by the manifestation of God.

And when the engagement was over, and they were returning again with joy, they recognised Nicanor lying dead in full armour; and there arose a shout and tumult, and then they blessed the Sovereign Lord in the language of their fathers. And he that in all things was in body and soul the foremost champion of his fellow-citizens, he that kept through life the good will of his youth toward his countrymen, commanded to cut off Nicanor's head, and his hand with the shoulder, and bring them to Jerusalem. And when he had arrived there, and had called his countrymen together and set the priests before the altar, he sent for them that were in the citadel; and shewing the head of the vile Nicanor, and the hand of that profane man, which with proud brags he had stretched out against the holy house of the Almighty, and cutting out the tongue of the impious Nicanor, he said that he would give it by pieces to the birds, and hang up the rewards of his madness over against the sanctuary. And they all looking up unto heaven blessed the Lord who had manifested himself, saying, Blessed be he that hath preserved his own place undefiled. And he hanged Nicanor's head and shoulder from the citadel, a sign, evident unto all and manifest, of the help of the Lord. And they all ordained with a common decree in no wise to let this day pass undistinguished, but to mark with honour the thirteenth day of the twelfth month (it is called Adar in the Syrian tongue), the day before the day of Mordecai.

This then having been the issue of the attempt of Nicanor, and the city having from those times been held by the Hebrews, I also will here make an end of my book. And if I have written well and to the point in my story, this is what I myself desired; but if meanly and indifferently, this is all I could attain unto. For as it is distasteful to drink wine alone, and in like manner again to drink water alone, while the mingling of wine with water at once giveth full pleasantness to the flavour; so also the fashioning of the language delighteth the ears of them that read the story.

And here shall be the end.

III MACCABEES

(First Century B.C.)

A NEW TRANSLATION AND INTRODUCTION
BY H. ANDERSON

Saved by a renegade Jew from a plot against his life by Theodotus, Ptolemy IV Philopator, King of Egypt (221-204 B.C.), decisively defeats Antiochus III the Great of Syria at Raphia (1: 1-5). He then visits neighboring cities, distributing gifts to their shrines and securing their loyalty (1:6f). A friendly delegation from the Jews persuades him to visit Jerusalem, where he is so impressed by the Temple that he longs to enter the sanctuary. His request causes a great furor in the city, but despite repeated remonstrances he is undeterred from his desire (1:8-29). The High Priest Simon, recalling God's wonderful deliverances of Israel in the past, prays that Ptolemy's threatened act of desecration might be averted, whereupon the king is punished by a stroke from God and falls on the ground in a swoon (2:1-22). On his return to Egypt, bent on revenge against the Jews, he decides to deprive them of their civil rights and to have them branded with the ivy leaf, the emblem of Dionysus. However, if any should participate in the cult of Dionysus they would enjoy the privileges of citizens of Alexandria (2:23-30). The majority of Jews resist gallantly, and the enraged king commands that all the Jews in Egypt, men, women, and children, be brought in chains to Alexandria and be put to death (2:31—3:30). Cruelly treated and herded together like animals on board ship, a great multitude are transported to the outskirts of Alexandria, where they are imprisoned in the racecourse (4:1-3). So vast is their number that the registration of their names takes forty days and cannot be completed because the supply of writing materials is exhausted (4:14-21). Ptolemy now orders that the Jews should be trampled by five hundred elephants, driven to fury by potent doses of wine and frankincense, but the king amazingly falls into a deep sleep so that the execution is postponed until the next day (5:1-22). The following day the Jews are once again spared their ordeal by a miraculous divine intervention which renders Ptolemy oblivious to his previous commands (5:23-35). Later the same day, however, he renews his instructions that the elephants should be made ready for the next morning (5:36-45). At dawn, when all is set and the king is already on his way with the panoplied beasts to the racecourse, the aged and esteemed Eleazar prays for God to intervene, and two angels, visible to all except the Jews, strike terror into the king and his troops and turn the elephants back upon the king's forces (5:46-6:21). The king, his disposition now totally transformed, is indignant with his counselors and orders not only that the Jews be released but that they celebrate a festival for seven days at his expense (6:22-30). So on the very spot where they had been doomed to die, the Jews feast and give thanks for their deliverance, and thereupon resolve that these days should be kept as a festival forever (6:30-41). In a letter to all governors in the provinces, the king now charges them to offer every protection to the Jews (7:1-9), and the Jews, having been granted permission to slay those of their brethren who had apostatized from the faith, do just that. They then institute another seven-day festival at Ptolemais and return in safety to their own homes (7:10-23).

Texts

Third Maccabees is not found in either Vaticanus or Sinaiticus, but does appear in the third great uncial manuscript of the Greek Bible, Alexandrinus, which dates from the middle part of the fifth century. The eighth or ninth century Codex Venetus also contains a text of 3 Maccabees which merits recognition alongside the Alexandrinus. In addition, there are a number of important minuscule manuscripts of 3 Maccabees. Somewhat less reliable, however, are those minuscules which stand in the textual tradition initiated by Lucian of Antioch (martyred A.D. 312), whose revision of the Septuagint became standard in Syria, Asia Minor, and Constantinople. The version of 3 Maccabees in the Syriac Peshitta (late 4th cent.) represents a free and expanded rendering, and is mainly Lucianic in character. There is also a rather paraphrastic Armenian version from some time between A.D. 400-600. The book does not stand in the Vulgate of Jerome (A.D.382-404) and so is neither in the Roman Catholic Bible nor in the Apocrypha of the Protestant churches.

On the whole the text of 3 Maccabees is in very good shape. The present translation is based on the edition by A. Rahlfs, *Septuaginta*, vol. 1 (Stuttgart, 1935). In the commentary only those variant readings are noted which substantially affect the meaning of a sentence or passage. A fuller critical apparatus is available in Rahlfs' *Septuaginta*, in H.B. Swete's *The Old Testament in Greek*, vol. 3 (Cambridge, 1899), and in R. Hanhart's *Maccabaeorum Liber III* (Sept. Gott. 9.3; Gottingen, 1960). The symbols used in the commentary are: A = Alexandrinus; V = Venetus; m = one minuscule; mm = more than one minuscule: L = the Lucianic recension; Syr. = Syriac Peshitta; Arm. = Armenian Version.

Original Language

All indication are that 3 Maccabees was first written in Greek. The work may be classed as an "historical romance," and as such it bears some resemblance to the Greek "romances" which flourished in the hellenistic period. Only a few of these, like the *Chaereas and Callirhoë* of Chariton, have survived, but 3 Maccabees shares enough features in common with them to suggest that its writer was acquainted with this type of literary model - the legendary embellishment of the career or of an episode in the career of an actual historical personage; a climactic scene describing the threatened destruction and miraculous deliverance of hero or heroine, generally in a public place such as the racecourse or theater; the prominence given to the religious element; the citation of putative letters or documents; the heightening of incidents in the story for dramatic effect by the addition of colorful but irrelevant detail.[1]

However, it is in the style and language employed that our author most of all exhibits his Greek hand. He often indulges in "fine writing," piling epithet upon epithet and participial clause upon participial clause. The book abounds in rhetorical repetitions and exaggerations. The vocabulary is rich and varied, and contains numerous pure classical forms as well as several which betray the influence of *koine* usage on the writer. He is acquainted also with words that occur only in Greek poetry and has distinct leaning toward compound verbs and adjectives, some of which he may even have coined himself since they are not found elsewhere in Greek literature, e.g. *bythotrephes̈* = "*sea* nurtured" (6:8), puropnous = "blazing" (6:34). All of this clearly stamps the author as a pseudo-classicist or pseudo- Atticist, at home with various phases of the Greek language.[2]

Date

Internal historical evidence points with certainty only to an upper and lower limit for the work. On the one side it begins with a brief depiction of the Battle of Raphia, which took place in 217 B.C. On the other side, in view of the glorification of the Jerusalem Temple in the book, the Temple is obviously still standing and the destruction that befell it in A.D. 70 has not yet occurred. Beyond that, further significant historical clues to a firmer dating within the period 217 B.C. - A.D. 70 are lacking. Josephus (Apion 2:5) gives a similar but much more sober account of the incident of the elephants, but unlike our author he attributes the outrage to a later Ptolemy, namely Ptolemy IX Physcon (146-117 B.C.). But Josephus is by no means necessarily correct in this. In fact, evidence has been adduced from the papyri to show that Physcon was favorably disposed toward the Jews.[3]

Accordingly, it does not follow that the author of 3 Maccabees must have written during or after Physcon's reign, or that he must knowingly have transferred the episode of the elephants to Philopator to suit his own polemic or apologetic purposes. Conceivably, since both Josephus and 3 Maccabees associate the story of the elephants with the institution of a particular festival, it may go back to some historical event. More probably Josephus' more restrained version and 3 Maccabees' more highly adorned version both stem from a popular legend which originated in the third century B.C. and which arose on the basis of the known fact that Egyptian monarchs made use of elephants for military purposes.[4] The story of the elephants, consequently, is a most uncertain criterion for dating 3 Maccabees.

It has been maintained that 3 Maccabees is a *Gelegenheitschrift*, that is a document produced in a specific set of historical circumstances and designed, like the apocalyptic writings, to aid people meet and overcome a particular crisis, in the case of 3 Maccabees obviously a crisis for the Jewish people. Ewald suggested that the crisis reflected in 3 Maccabees is the persecution of Alexandrian Jews during the reign of the Roman Emperor Caligula and that the book is connected with his attempt to set up his image in the Jerusalem Temple in A.D. 40.[5] But if the author of 3 Maccabees wrote under Caligula and cloaked his criticism of Caligula's administration under the record of an analogous crisis in the reign of Philopator of Egypt in the distant past, we should surely expect some hint of the most sinister and oppressive features, the imperial claim to divine honors (especially since the Ptolemies, too, were *theoi* or "gods") and the desecration of sanctuaries by attempts to erect imperial effigies in them. But there is no such hint!

More recently M. Hadas has argued that 3 Maccabees was written in response to a crisis affecting Egyptian Jews when Egypt was made a Roman province in a 24 B.C. and the Jews' civic status was jeopardized by the new Roman administration.[6] The hinge of his argument on the historical side is that 3 Maccabees 2:28 refers to a *laographia* which, as 2:30 indicated, here means the "poll tax" of the Roman period (liability to it involving loss of citizen status), and that this accords with the administrative situation just after the Romans took over in Egypt. On the other hand, it has been proposed that Philopator himself may have been responsible for the institution of a poll tax in Egypt,[7] although the ostraca of the Ptolemaic period appear to suggest that no general poll tax was applied in early Ptolemaic Egypt similar to the Roman laographia.[8] However, the term does occur in Ptolemaic papyri in the less technical sense of a "registry of taxable *laoi*." And it is likely that, in view of the heavy expenses incurred for his realm in two wars, Philopator enforced a much stricter collection of rents, taxes, and arrears.[9] Also the old salt tax, levied on every inhabitant of Egypt, was, as Rostovtzeff notes,[10] virtually equivalent to a poll tax, and the fact that certain privileged classes could be exempted from it by royal command implies a caste system of taxation under which the Jews could have suffered at any time during the Ptolemaic period. Accordingly, the mention of *laographia* and what it may have implied in 3 Maccabees 2:28, 30 is hardly sufficient in and by itself to constrain us to date the work in the Roman period.

The Achilles heel of every theory of dating that would trace 3 Maccabees to a specific moment of trial and tribulation in the history of Egyptian Jews is that the book itself does not really read like a "crisis document." Among the favorite themes of the apocalyptic writings are retribution, life after death, the last judgement, and the impending cataclysmic overthrow of the existing world order through God's ushering in the end-time. Such themes are conspicuous by their absence from 3 Maccabees.[11] In fact, glad thanksgiving for God's merciful deliverances of his people and festival joy feature quite prominently in the work, and the sense of an inevitably happy outcome that runs through it might the more imply an era of success and prosperity for the Jews when it was written.[12] On the whole it is best regarded as an edifying and apologetic tract of a generalizing kind, designed to keep the lamp of orthodox Jewish faith burning, to exhibit the loyalty of Jews as subject people in the territories of their sojourn, and to account etiologically for the observance of a particular Egyptian Jewish festival.

Literary characteristics and relationships of 3 Maccabees offer more promising leads than internal historical evidence toward a narrower dating within the period 200 B.C.-A.D. 70. Third Maccabees 6:6 reveals the author's acquanintance with the Greek additions to the Book of Daniel, and since Daniel itself is normally ascribed to the beginning of the Maccabean period, around 165 B.C., this points to a time for 3 Maccabees hardly earlier than the latter part of the first century B.C. In 3 Maccabees 3:12 and 7:1 there occurs a formula of salutation in the style *chairein kai errōsthai* = "greetings and good health." The same formula occurs also in the Letter of Aristeas, the normally accepted date for which is around 100 B.C. And the fact that the papyri of an earlier and later period attest different formulas of salutation tends to confirm that the "greetings and good health" of 3 Maccabees and the Letter of Aristeas was the favored usage about the turn of the first century B.C.

On a broader front, the association of 3 Maccabees in style and content with 2 Maccabees and the Letter of Aristeas support a date early in the first century for our book. Similarities of vocabulary, some of it relatively rare elsewhere, and of phrase between 2 and 3 Maccabees are striking. In both works the same motifs are prominent (see Relation to Apocryphal Books), and especially noteworthy is the resemblance between the narrative of the miracle by which punishment was visited on Ptolemy in 3 Maccabees 2:21-24 and the narrative concerning Heliodorus in 2 Maccabees 3:22-31. The correspondences between 2 and 3 Maccabees are scarcely comprehensive enough to suggest they were written by a single author, but they are close enough to suggest that the two authors shared the same thought world and most probably wrote at approximately the same time. The consensus is that 2 Maccabees can hardly be earlier than the last quarter of the second century B.C.[13] To judge from the literary traits and connections of 3 Maccabees, a date in the earlier part of the first century B.C. commends itself as a reasonable hypothesis.

Provenance

The main in action in the "plot" of 3 Maccabees takes place in the neighborhood of Alexandria in Egypt. Throughout, one of the author's primary concerns is with the status of Egyptian Jews. His work, in its pseudo-classicism, shares the Alexandrian flavor of 2 Maccabees and the Letter of Aristeas and shows the same familiarly not only with the court life of the Ptolemies but with the technical language of official Ptolemaic decrees. The lines of evidence converge on Alexandria as the place of origin of 3 Maccabees.

Historical Importance

The title "Third Maccabees" is a misnomer for our document. The events described in it antedate the Maccabean period proper by some fifty years or more. By any standard the book has an abrupt introduction, even more noticeable in the Greek than in English translation. Moreover, the plot of Theodotus is introduced in the 1:2 as though it were already known to the reader. From this it has sometimes been deduced that the work as we have it is truncated and originally contained an introductory chapter or chapters in which, among other things, the author would have explained how he intended to produce an appropriate prolegomenon to the epic struggle of the Maccabees. But any attempt to reconstruct the contents of a supposedly lost chapter or chapters is of necessity purely conjectural. Most probably our document received its title through its collection with 1 and 2 Maccabees in the manuscripts or perhaps because its theme, the sacrilegious intent of Ptolemy and the brave Jewish reaction, was felt to have an affinity with later imperial arrogance and heroic Jewish resistance in the days of the Maccabean revolt.

Whatever the case may be, more suitable for 3 Maccabees that the designation *Makkabaika* would be *Ptolemaika*, the heading under which the Letter of Aristeas was listed by Syncellus (I.516), the Byzantine historian, around A.D. 800. But even as Ptolemaika, 3 Maccabees adds little to our knowledge of actual events around 217 B.C. in the reign of Ptolemy IV Philopator. Our author's brief portrayal of Philopator's victory at Raphia in that year (1:1-7) differs only in detail from the description in Poplybius (5). In the latter, for example, the opposing armies arrive at Raphia about the same time, Arsinoë joins Philopator in exhorting his army to gallantry before the battle, and while Theodotus and his plot against Ptolemy are mentioned there is no reference to the Dositheus of 3 Maccabees 1:3. But beyond these first few verses, as far as the provision of reliable historical information on the several separate incidents related goes, 3 Maccabees takes us into very uncertain territory indeed. While there is no *a priori* reason why Philopator should not have visted Jerusalem after his triumph at not-so-distant Raphia in the south of Palestine, the story of his encounter with the Jews at the Jerusalem Temple is told in which highly legendary terms as to cast grave suspicion on the factuality of the whole episode. The account of the "elephant outrage" most likely stems, as we have noted, from a popular legend which circulated during the last two centuries B.C. And the narrative of the cruel deportation of Jews from their homes to the vast concourse of the hippodrome at Alexandria is so overdrawn as also to savor of the legendary.

Nevertheless, 3 Maccabaees clearly reflects a sound general knowledge on its writer's part of the life and times of Ptolemy IV. From his depiction of the Battle of Raphia, consistent in its main lines with that of Polybius, it may reasonably be inferred that he had access to some relatively trustworthy source, possibly the lost history of Ptolemy Meglopolitanus. Polybius himself alludes to this Ptolemy, but only a few fragments of his work survive and are to be found in Müller's *Fragmenta 3.66*[14] However, aside from the opening verses on Raphia, our author reveals an undoubted acquaintance with the conditions prevailing in Egypt under Philopator. The characterization of Philopator in *3* Maccabees is true to what is known of him from elsewhere: his love of banqueting, his openness to the whims of his courtiers, his hope of uniting Jews and Greeks in the worship of his ancestor Dionysus, prompted possibly by the contemporary identification of Dionysus' name Sabazius with the Jewish Sabaoth.[15] Also, our author's familiarity with the style and format of official Ptolemaic letters or decrees is generally conceded.

We possess all too little information about the historical circumstances of the Jews in Egypt during the

Ptolemaic period, and 3 Maccabaees is to be sure of broad historical value. Nevertheless, the writer is not an historian whose first interest is to record accurately what happened or to preserve the memory of past events simply for their own sake. He is, rather, a man of orthodox Jewish religious sentiment who employs the medium of historical narration, albeit a narration which he has greatly romanticized, in order, on the one hand, to edify and encourage the faithful within the fold of his own people and, on the other hand, to commend them to outsider as a "special people" and to defend and justify their mode and quality of life, their religious sensitivities, and their continuing religious observances.

Theological importance

Our author's theological standpoint can in some measure be gauged as much from what he omits to say as from what he actually does say in his narrative. There is no trace of any of the leading motifs which permeate the apocalyptic writings that began to flourish in the earlier part of the second century B.C. For example, missing are ideas regarding life beyond death, retribution, the last judgment, the messianic hope, and the dawning of the new age. The absence of such themes is all the more remarkable in as much as the martyrology of 2 Maccabees, which our author probably knew, testifies extensively to the notion of a just redress for the martyred dead in the afterlife. Moreover, there is no suggestion in 3 Maccabees of the "liberation of reason"[16] or process of secularization, the radical questioning of skepticism typical of such products of the wisdom literature of later Israel as Proverbs, Job, and Ecclesiastics. Nor again, although our author is a neo-classicist, probably from Alexandria, and presumably familiar with Platonic ideas, is there any hint of the Alexandrian drift toward Philo's attempted fusion of Greek thought with the Torah or his allegorical method of scriptural exegesis.

Over against apocalyptic, wisdom, and hellenistic philosophy, our author may best be pictured as a staunch conservative, swimming against the stream of the more radical tendencies of his time. In fact, he appears as an ardent champion of the old Deuteronomic orthodoxy, which at the risk of oversimplification may be described as the conviction that God rewards the righteous and punishes the wicked, and against which the author of Job registers a vehement protest. In 3 Maccabees the God who intervenes wonderfully to save his people is very much the God of the faithful and the just. Ptolemy IV does not at all subscribe to the worship of the God of Israel, but in his letter to his generals he is represented as acknowledging officially that the Jews are a "peculiar people": And knowing of a surety that God in heaven protects the Jews, in alliance with them continually, like a father with his children.. . Be sure of this, if we devise any evil scheme against them or cause them any trouble, we shall have not man, but the Most High God, who is ruler of all power, as our adversary to exact vengeance for what is done, inexorably in all circumstances and for all time: (7:6, 9). Our author gives no sign at all of being possessed of any proselytizing zeal or of moving beyond the particularism of which the pagan Philopator is here made the eloquent spokesman.

Third Maccabees strongly reflects its writer's unshakable hold upon the faith of earlier Israel that God continually moved toward her in her history and actively participated in it, ruling, controlling, and directing her way, and this at a period when such a faith had been trenchantly questioned by more adventurous spirits in Judaism. The prayers of the High Priest Simon in 2:2-20 and of Eleazar in 6:2-15 are in effect celebrations of "sacred history," reminiscent of those Psalms (e.g. 78, 80, 106, 114, 135, 136) which sing Yahweh's praises for his former acts of deliverance. However, the manner in which our author extends the line of "sacred history" into the time of Ptolemy IV might appear to be somewhat naive - his reports on the miraculous divine interferences by which Ptolemy and his officials were thwarted of their designs against the Jews may hardly be described as strong on historical realism. But in recounting them he does enter, however remotely, into the ancient Hebrew tradition of the holy wars in which Yahweh fought for and rescued his people, a concept which reappears in new forms in the prophets (cf. e.g. Isa 29:6, 8; 30:30).[17] And he is at least sophisticated enough theologically to recognize that the Jews do not require visible, cosmic signs to support their faith in Yahweh's marvelous interventions on their behalf: He is, in fact, at pains to affirm that the "two angels" who occasion a dramatic reversal of fortunes at the racecourse were "visible to all except the Jews" (6:18).

In other salient aspects of his theological demeanor, our author subscribes without question to ancient Jewish norms. He has a strong sense of vast distance between the "sacred" and the "secular," and this shows particularly in his reverence for the Temple, which he needs only to call "the place" in the assumption that his readers will understand. The rather extravagant description of 1:19-29 reveals how much for him the Temple is filled with the numinous. And the ultimate in nefarious deeds is Ptolemy Philopator's sacrilegious intent to enter the Temple. Prominent also is the writer's rigorous devotion to the Law, nowhere more in evidence than in his report (and tacit endorsement) of the slaying of over three hundred renegade Jews, in accordance with the injunctions of Deuteronomy 13:6-18.

Again, the niceties of strict religious observance carry a special appeal for our author. He shares with hellenistic Judaism the tendency to pile up reverential epithets on every mention of the name of God (see e.g. 2:2-21; 5:7; 6:2-9, 18, 28) and even employs some titles not used elsewhere in the Septuagint *(e.g. monarchos, 2:2; propator, 2:21; megalokrator, 6:2; misoubris, 6:9).* He subscribes to the view that the efficacy of prayer is related to the attitude or quality of life of the petitioner: Witness his description of the high priest's assuming the correct posture in 2:1 and of the exalted status of the aged Eleazar in 6:1. For him clearly "the heartfelt prayer of a good man works very powerfully" (Jas 5:16). Finally, part at least of our writer's motivation for telling his story was to compose a "festival legend" for a feast celebrated among Egyptian Jews in his own time, perhaps an Egyptian counterpart of the Feast of Purim, to which the Book of Esther testifies and which probably originated in the eastern Diaspora.[18]

Relation to canonical books

The writer of 3 Maccabees does not seem to have been influence especially by any particular canonical work. Rather he appears to have been steeped in the old biblical traditions, a selection of which he has drawn upon in somewhat random fashion, notably in the prayers he put on the lips of Simon and Eleazar in chapters 2 and 4 respectively. However, his work does bear a resemblance, at one or two points, to the Hebrew Book of Ester. There, as in 3 Maccabees, a foreign tyrant plans the destruction of the Jewish people in his territory, but his (Haman's) plot is thwarted and the Jews are authorized by King Ahasuerus to turn against and stamp out their enemies (Esth 8:3-14). Nevertheless, the differences between the two books are much more notable than the similarities. Esther is a secular pamphlet which attributes the deliverance of the Jews to human agency, in short the wiles of the heroine Esther, and never even mentions God or prayers to God. Third Maccabees has no hero proper but subordinates everything to God, who intervenes to save his people. Moreover, unlike 3 Maccabees, Esther has nothing at all to say on the subject of the loyalty of the Jews as a subject people. Accordingly, it is by no means certain that there is any direct line of connection between the Hebrew Esther and 3 Maccabees, nor can it be said with any degree of assurance that our author set out purposely to correct the secular tone of Esther.[19]

Relation to apocryphal books

Third Maccabees has points of contact most of all with 2 Maccabees and the Letter of Aristeas (see Date). Second Maccabees contains a number of leading incidents and ideas which parallel those in 3 Maccabees. Second Maccabees tells of the repulse of Heliodorus' attempt to profane the Temple (3:22-3 1), and the punishment visited upon Antiochus for his arrogance (2Mac 9:4ff.) is like Philopator's (3Mac 2:21 - 24). The awesomeness of the Temple (2Mac; 3:15-22; 8:2-4; 14:34-36; 3Mac 1:11-16;2:1-21); portentous visions (2Mac 3:25; 10:29; 11:8; 3Mac; 6:18); attacks upon religion (2Mac 6:9; 3Mac; 2:27-33; 3:21); efforts to impose an alien citizenship (2Mac 4:9; 3Mac 2:27-30); memorial festivals (2Mac 10:6; 15:36; 3Mac 6:30-36); the appearance of the esteemed Eleazar (2Mac

6:1, 16), and the horror of the Jewish populace (2Mac 3:15ff.; 3Mac 1:16-29; 4:3-8) are all prominent features of both works. The resemblance of 3 Maccabees to the Letter of Aristeas is hardly any less close. Both books exalt the Jews and extol their loyalty as subjects of the Ptolemies. In both, a Ptolemy acknowledges that God is the special protector of his own people (LetAris 16, 19, 37; 3Mac 3:21; 5:31, 6:24-28; 7:6-9). Both glory in the inextinguishable majesty of the Temple (LetAris 83-91; 99; 3Mac 1: 11-16; 2:1-21), and stress the "apartness" of the Jews in food and life (LetAris 128-66, 3Mac 3:3-7) while at the same time making much of Egyptian royal feast (LetAris 187, etc.; 3Mac 4:16, etc.). Perhaps even more significant is the fact that our author uses a relatively large number of words and expressions that are found in 2 Maccabees and/or the Letter of Aristeas but are rare elsewhere and in many cases do not occur at all in the Septuagint.[20] Resemblances of terminology in the official letters and decrees recorded in each work are especially striking.

Not surprisingly, therefore, the direct literary dependence of 3 Maccabees on 2 Maccabees and the Letter of Aristeas has been argued. But the reverse has also been argued with just as much cogency, and if each document is examined as a whole and full account is taken of the differences as well as the similarities, the safest conclusion is simply that the authors belonged to the same milieu and in particular shared a common stock of knowledge of official Egyptian procedures and of the technical language of Egyptian royal decrees and letters.

Cultural Importance

As far as can be gathered, the story told in 3 Maccabees has had no influence at all on the art or literature, secular or religious, of the West. Missing from Jerome's Vulgate, its chances of even becoming known were slender indeed. But even in the East, 3 Maccabees has left remarkably few traces. In one of his exegetical works, commenting on Daniel 11, Theodoret of Antioch (c. A.D. 393-c. 458), who became Bishop of Cyrrhus in Syria, offers a brief summary of 3 Maccabees, and the existence of an old Syriac translation implies a more general interest in the work on the part of the Syrian Church.

SELECT BIBLIOGRAPHY

Charlesworth, PMR, pp. 149-51
Delling, *Bibliographie, pp. 146f.*

Eissfeldt, O. *The Old Testament; An Introduction.* Trans. P. R. Ackroyd, New York and Evanston, 1965: pp. 581f.
Emmet, C. W. "The Third Book of Maccabees," *APOT*; vol. 1, pp. 156-73.
Hadas, M. *The Third and Fourth Books of Maccabees.* New York, 1953.
Rostovtzeff, M. "Ptolemaic Egypt," *The Cambridge Ancient History,* Cambridge, 1964; vol. 7, pp. 109-54.
Schurer, E. *History.* Div. 2, vol. 3, pp. 216-19.
Tarn, W. W. "The Struggle of Egypt Against Syria and Macedonia,: *The Cambridge Ancient History.* Cambridge, 1964; vol. 7, pp. 699-731.
Weiser, A. *The Old Testament: Its Formation and Development.* Trans. D. M. Barton. New York, 1961: pp. 395-97.

THE THIRD BOOK OF MACCABEES

Ptolemy IV Philopator's victory at Raphia

1. **1** From people returning from the scene Philopator
received the news of Antiochus' capture of the places
which had been under his control. He then put out
orders to all his infantry and cavalry forces and
moved on, taking his sister Arsinoe along with him,
to the territory around Raphia[a] where Antiochus'
army was camped. Dan 11: 11f.
2. But a certain Theodotus[b] decided to carry out a
scheme he had in mind, so he took some of the very
best of Ptolemy's soldiers who had previously been
placed in his charge and went across by night to
Ptolemy's tent intending to kill him
3. single-handedly and end the war at a stroke.
However, one Dositheos, called the son of Drimylus,
who was a Jew by birth but later had renounced the
Law and abandoned his ancestral beliefs, removed
Ptolemy and had a poor unknown fellow sleep in his
tent bed instead, and he of course suffered the fate
intended for
4. Ptolemy. A violent battle ensued, and when the tide
ran in favor of Antiochus, Arsinoe traversed the ranks
and, wailing and in tears, with her braided hair hanging loose, begged them to take courage and rally not
just for their own sake but for the sake of their wives
and children; she even promised to give each one
5. of them, if they won, two minae of gold.[d]
The outcome was that the enemy was destroyed in
the combat and many also were taken prisoner.

Ptolemy visits Jerusalem and determines to enter the Temple

6. With the plot against him thwarted, Ptolemy now
decided to visit the neighboring
7. cities and offer them encouragement. When he had
done this and distributed
8. gifts to their shrines, he made his subjects feel secure.[e]
When the Jews sent a delegation of the council and
the elders to greet him and offer him friendly gifts
and congratulate him on his achievements, he was all
the more eager to visit them
9. as soon as possible. So he came to Jerusalem, where
he sacrificed to God the Greatest and put up thank
offerings, observing to some extent the proprieties of
the place. When he entered the sacred place[f] he was
struck by its immaculate and
10. dignified appearance 2Mac 3:36; 1:16; 3:11; 4:16; 5:25; 7:22
and, marveling at the orderliness of the Temple, asked
11. himself thoughtfully whether he should go into the
sanctuary. They told him that this was quite improper since not even the Jewish people themselves were
allowed in nor indeed any and every priest but only
the high priest, who was the chief of
12. all, and he only once a year. However, he was not at
all convinced. Even after the Law had been read out
to him he persistently affirmed that he must enter and
13. said, "Even if they are deprived of this honor, I must
not be." Ex 30:10; Lev 16:34 He then asked why it was
that when he entered every (other) shrine nobody
present stopped
14. him. All too hastily somebody said that it was wrong
to speak of this as if it
15. were a marvel. "Even so," he said, "why should I not
enter in my case whether
16 they want me to or not?" Then the priests in all their
vestments prostrated themselves and entreated
Almighty God to help them in their present difficulty and make their assailant change his mind, and they
filled the Temple with loud cries and tears.

The rush of the outraged citizenry to the Temple

17. The people who were left in the city hurried out
in disarray, reckoning that
18. something mysterious was going on. 2Mac 3:15-22 Even
the young women who had been confined to their
chambers rushed out with their mothers, and they
took dust and covered their hair with it and filled the
streets with cries of grief and moans.
19. Those recently married left the chambers where the
marriage bed had been prepared and, heedless of the
modesty appropriate to their station, ran about in disorder
20. in the city. 4:6 The mothers and nurses in charge of
the youngest children left them here and there, in
houses or in the streets, and, abandoning all caution,
thronged
21. to the most glorious Temple. Many and varied were
the prayers of those who
22. gathered there because of the king's sacrilegious
designs. At the same time the bolder spirits among the
citizens would not endure the pressure he was exerting
23. to gain his own ends or his determination to carry
through his project and, sounding a call to take up
arms with all haste and to die bravely for the Law of
their fathers, they caused a great disturbance in the
place. Only with difficulty were they dissuaded by
the elders, and they then joined them in the posture of
24 25 prayer. Meanwhile the multitude went on with
their prayers as previously. But the elders close to the
king tried in many ways to divert his mind from the
26. scheme he had so arrogantly conceived. With great
boldness he dismissed every plea, however, and, bent
on achieving his declared purpose, was already moving
27. forward. When those around him saw what was hap-
pening they joined our own people in calling on him who
is all-powerful to help them in their present extremity

28. and not overlook this insolent act of lawlessness. The
combined shouts of the
29. crowd, ceaseless and vehement, caused an indescribable uproar. It seemed as if not only the people but the very walls and the whole pavement cried out, so much at that moment did they all prefer death to the profanation of the Temple.

The prayer of Simon the High Priest

1. **2** The high priest, Simon, knelt in homage in front of
the sanctuary and, holding
2. out his hands with due reverence, he prayed. Pss 105,106 6:1-15 "LORD, LORD, King of heaven, ruler of all creation, holy among the holy ones, sovereign, conqueror of all, pay heed to us who are sorely vexed by a wicked and corrupt man, reckless in his
3. effrontery and might. For you who created all things
and govern the whole world
4. are a just ruler and condemn all who act insolently and arrogantly. You destroyed men for their wicked deeds in the past, among them giants relying on their own strength and self-confidence, upon whom you brought an immeasurable flood of
5. water. Gen 6:4-7; Jdt 16:7; Sir 16:7; WisSol 14:6; Gen 7 When the inhabitants of Sodom acted insolently and became notorious for their crimes you burned them up with fire and brimstone and made them an
6. example to later generations. Gen 19:24 You tested the proud Pharaoh, who enslaved your holy people Israel, with many different punishments and made known to him your
7. mighty power. Ex 5-12 When he pursued with chariots a great host of people, you overwhelmed him in the depths of the sea and brought safely through those who

8. believed on you, the ruler of all creation. Ex 14:21-31
When they saw the works of your hand
9. they praised you, conqueror of all. You, king, when
you created the boundless and measureless earth,
chose this city and sanctified this Temple for your
name, though you lack nothing at all, and you glorified it by a splendid manifestation
10. and established it to the glory of your great and honorable name. Ex 15 And in your love for the house of
Israel you promised that, if ever we should turn away
or distress overtake us, and we came to this holy
place to pray, you would hear our
11 12 prayer. And you are surely faithful and true to your
word. Seeing that often when our forefathers were
afflicted you helped them in their humiliation and
13. rescued them from great ills, so look now, holy king,
when we are oppressed and subjected to our enemies
on account of our many serious sins and are weak
14. and resourceless. In our calamity this arrogant and
corrupt man sets out to violate
15. the holy place which is dedicated on earth to the
name of your glory. Your
16. dwelling place, the heaven of heaven, is beyond the
reach of men. But since you sanctified this holy place
because you took pleasure in your glory among your
17. people Israel, 1Kgs 8:27-29 do not punish us by the
uncleanness of these men, nor censure us by their
corruption, lest the lawless ones boast in their wrath
or exult in the
18. insolence of their tongue, saying, 'We have trodden
down the house of the
19. sanctuary as the houses of the abominations are trodden down.' 1Mac 6:7 Wipe out our
20. sins and disperse our offenses and show your pity at
this moment. Let your mercies speedily overtake us,
and let praises fill the mouths of those who are fallen
and crushed in their souls, and grant us peace."

God's punishment of Ptolemy and the king's vengeful response

21. Then the God who beholds all, the supremely holy father among the holy, heard the prayer of supplication offered in the regular form and scourged the one who
22. was greatly exalted by his own insolence and effrontery,Deut 32:6; Isa 63:16 tossing him to and fro like a reed on the wind until he fell impotent to the ground, with his limbs paralyzed and unable to speak, completely overpowered by a righteous judgment.
2Mac 3:22-30; 9:4-10
23. When his friends and members of his bodyguard saw how severe was the chastisement that overtook him, they were afraid he might die, and, smitten with
24. extreme alarm, they pulled him out. However, punished though he had been, when he recovered shortly after he was by no means contrite but went away with
25. bitter threats. Thereafter, on his arrival in Egypt, he became even more extravagant in his wickedness through his aforementioned boon companions and friends,
26. complete strangers to everything that was just, and not only was he not satisfied with his innumerable excesses, he even reached such a pitch of arrogance as to concoct slanderous reports in these regions. Many of his friends watched the
27. king's procedure intently and themselves fell into line with his wishes. His aim was to bring disgrace upon the nation publicly. Accordingly, he erected a pillar
28. on the tower at the palace and inscribed on it,"That none of those who did not sacrifice should be permitted to enter their temples, and that all Jews should be required to enroll in the census and be reduced to the condition of slaves, and

29. that any who spoke against it should be taken by
force and put to death, that those who were enrolled
should be branded by fire on their bodies with an ivy
leaf, the emblem of Dionysus, and should be registered according to their former
30. restricted status. 2Mac 6:1; LetAris 22 But so as not to
appear to be an enemy to them all he added, "But if
any of them prefer to join those who are initiated in
the mysteries, they
31. would be on the same footing as the citizens of
Alexandria." Some who objected strongly to the
price the city had to pay for the practice of its religion
surrendered gladly, expecting to participate in some
of the prestige that would come from
32. association with the king. But most resisted with gallantry of spirit and did not abandon their religious
practice, but they gave their money as a ransom for
their
33. life and fearlessly sought to save themselves from the
enrollment. They persisted in the hope that they
would obtain relief and despised those who left their
ranks, judging them to be enemies of the nation and
depriving them of any part in community life and
service.

The Jews in society

1. **3** On receiving word of this, the impious king was so
enraged he was not angry only with those who lived
in Alexandria but was even more bitterly opposed to
those in the country and ordered that all of them
should be assembled with haste
2. in one spot and put to death in the most violent way.
4:12 While this was being organized, a malicious
rumor was noised abroad against the Jewish nation
by men who conspired to harm them and grasped an

opportunity that arose to represent
3. them as hindering them from observance of their
laws. Esth 3:8 The Jews, however, steadily maintained
their goodwill toward the kings and their unwavering
loyalty.
4. But reverencing God and conducting themselves
according to his Law, they kept themselves apart in
the matter of food, and for this reason they appeared
hateful
5. to some. 4Mac; LetAris 128-66 They adorned their community life with the excellent practice of
6. righteousness and so established a good reputation
among all men. But of this excellent practice, which
was common talk everywhere regarding the Jewish
7. nation, the foreigners took no account whatever.
Instead they talked incessantly about how different
they were in regard to worship and food, asserting
that they did not fulfill their contracted obligations
either to the king or the armed forces but were hostile
and very unsympathetic to his interests. So it was no
small charge
8. they fastened on them. When the Greeks in the city,
who were in no way wronged by them, noticed the
unexpected tumult around these people, and the
unforeseen concourses taking place, they were
unable to help, for they lived under a tyranny, but
they did give them encouragement and felt sorry for
them, and
9. they assumed that things would change for the better.
4:1 Surely a community so
10. large that had done no wrong could not be left to such
a fate. Some of their neighbors and friends and business associates took some Jews aside secretly and
pledged to support them and make every effort to
assist them.

Ptolemy's decree that all Jews in his kingdom be arrested

11. The king, priding himself on his present prosperity and with no regard for the power of the Almighty God, and supposing that he could persist forever with the
12 same scheme, wrote the following letter against the Jews: 2:28-31; 1:9,16; 4:16; 5:25; 7:22 "King
13. Ptolemy Philopator, to his generals in Egypt and elsewhere, greeting and good health. I
14. myself am in good health and our affairs are prospering. Our expedition in Asia, of which you yourselves are aware, having been brought, as we expected, to its
15. successful conclusion with the deliberate help of the gods, we thought we would foster the inhabitants of Coele-Syria and Phoenicia, not by force of arms, but by
16. kindness and great benevolence, conferring benefits on them willingly. And having allotted very large revenues to the temples in the various cities, we proceeded also to Jerusalem, having gone up to do honor to the Temple of this accursed
17. people who never desist from their folly. Outwardly they seemed to welcome our presence, but in fact their welcome was insincere, for when we desired to
18. enter their shrine and to honor it with resplendent and beautiful offerings, carried away by their ancient pride, they stopped us from going in, but because of the benevolence we practice toward all men they were left untouched by our might.
19. But they plainly exhibited their hostility to us and, the only ones among all peoples who offer lordly resistance to kings and their own benefactors, they refused
20. to accept anything as genuine. For our part we accommodated ourselves to their folly, and returning victoriously to Egypt, we met all nations with benevolence:

21 we have acted rightly. Similarly, we made known to
all our readiness to forgive the Jews' fellow countrymen, because of their alliance with us and the many
affairs that had been entrusted to them from of old,
and we boldly decided to introduce a change, declaring them worthy of Alexandrian citizenship and
allowing
22. them to participate in our regular religious rites. 5:31; LetAris 36; 6:25; 7:7 But they misinterpreted us and
23. in their innate feelings of hostility rejected this good
offer. Inclining as they always do toward the mean
and petty, they not only rejected the invaluable citizenship, but also by their silence as well as by their
words they show contempt for the few among them
who are properly disposed to us, constantly nursing
the secret hope that with their disgraceful conduct we
would quickly alter our policy.
24. Accordingly, we have adequate proof of our conviction that these people are in every way hostile to us,
and noting in advance that, if ever a sudden disturbance should be stirred up against us later on, we
would have these impious people
25. behind our backs as traitors and barbarous enemies,
we have decreed that the very moment this letter
reaches you, you shall dispatch to us those who
reside among you, together with their women and
children, committing atrocities against them and
binding them fast all over in iron chains, to meet a
desperate and
26. ignominious death as befits traitorous foes. Ex 1:10
For we believe that when they are all punished
together, our government will be perfectly established forever in the
27. most secure and healthy condition. Whoever shelters
any Jews, from the old to the child and even to the
infant at the breast, shall with all his household be done
28. to a violent death with the most horrible torture.

Whoever wishes may act as informer, and he shall
receive the estate of the person who is sentenced to
punishment as well as two thousand drachmas from
the royal treasury and shall
29. also be rewarded with freedom. Any place where a
Jew is detected under any kind of shelter shall be
made out of bounds and burned with fire and shall
become
30. altogether useless for every mortal creature for all
time." Such was the form of the letter that was written.

The deportation of the Jews and their imprisonment at Alexandria

1. **4** In every place where the decree reached, a feast
was arranged for the heathen at the public expense
with noisy celebrations and gladness, with the hatred
which had long before become inveterate in their
hearts now being given open expression. Esth 4:3
2. But among the Jews there was incessant grief and
cries of lamentation with tears, and their hearts were
all aflame as they groaned and bewailed the unexpected
3. destruction so suddenly decreed against them. What
district or city or town or village with any inhabitants
at all or what streets were not filled with
4. lamentation and wailing for them? For with such vin-
dictive and pitiless spirit were they sent away, all of
them together, by the generals of the various cities,
that even some of their enemies, confronted with
their extraordinary suffering, and perceiving the people's pity for them and reflecting on life's strange
vicissitudes, were moved to
5. tears at their wretched expulsion. For there was taken
away a large company of old men, their heads cov-

ered with gray, and though their feet were sluggish
and crooked from age, they were having to force
themselves to a brisk pace under the
6. altogether shameless and relentless driving. The
young women who had but recently entered the
bridal chamber for the society of married life
exchanged their joy for wailing, and, with their per-
fume-drenched locks covered in dust. they were carried away unveiled and all joined in singing a dirge
instead of a wedding
7. hymn, as if torn asunder by the brutal mangling of the
heathen. And in full view of everybody they were
forcibly dragged along in bonds until they were
embarked
8. on board ship. Their husbands, in the full bloom of
youth, their necks girded with halters in place of gar-
lands, spent the remaining days of their wedding festival not in glad celebration and youthful recreation
but in dirges, seeing the grave
9. already yawning at their very feet. They were put on
board like animals, driven along under the constraint
of iron bonds. Some had their necks fastened to the
10. ship's benches, and others had their feet secured in
unbreakable fetters. Worse still, they were placed in
total darkness that they might be treated as traitors
11. throughout the voyage. When they had been brought
to the place called Schedia and the voyage as determined by the king was over, he ordered them to be
thrown into the hippodrome on the outskirts of the
city, an immense concourse eminently suitable for
making the captives a public example to all who
came down to the city and to those who left the city
for a sojourn in the country, the purpose being to prevent them from associating with the king's forces or
claiming to be within the
12. precincts of the city. When this was done, the king
heard that their fellow

13. countrymen came out frequently to bewail the bitter
fate of their brethren and in a rage ordered that they
should be treated in precisely the same way as the
others and should be allowed no remission whatever
of the punishment meted out to
14. these others. Moreover, the whole race was to be registered by name, not for the toilsome labor service,
briefly explained above, but to be tortured by the torments which he had commanded and to be put to
death in the space of a single
15. day. The registration, undertaken with shameful haste
and unremitting diligence from sunrise to sunset, was
closed after forty days, although still incomplete.
16. Filled with great and continuous joy, the king
appointed feasts at all his idol shrines, with a heart far
removed from the truth and a profane mouth, praising dumb objects unable to answer or help, and uttering improper words against the
17. Almighty God. After the interval of time mentioned
previously, the scribes reported to the king that they
could no longer continue the registration of the Jews
18. on account of their incalculable number, although in
fact the majority were still in the country, some still
remaining in their homes and others on the journey;
19. the task was impossible for all the generals in Egypt.
After threatening them harshly on the ground that
they had been bribed to contrive their escape, he was
20. eventually clearly convinced on this point when they
stated, with proof to back it up, that the paper mill
and the pens they used for writing had already given
21. out. But this was the working out of the invincible
providence of the one who helps the Jews from heaven.

The divine frustration of the king's plan to execute the Jews

1. **5** He then summoned Hermon, who was in charge of

the elephants, and,
2. filled with stern anger and rage and completely inflexible, ordered him for the following day to drug all the elephants, five hundred in number, with large handfuls of frankincense and quantities of unmixed wine, then when they were wild with the
3. plentiful supply of drink to bring them in to compass the fate of the Jews. When he had given out these orders he turned to his feasting, having brought together
4. those of his friends and army who were especially hostile to the Jews. Meanwhile, Hermon, the superintendent of the elephants, carried out his orders to the letter.
5. The attendants assigned for the purpose went out in the evening and bound the hands of the poor unfortunate people and took every other precaution to see that they were secure through the night, imagining that the whole nation would meet
6. its ruinous end in one blow. But the Jews, who seemed to the heathen to be bereft of every support, completely restricted as they were by their bonds, called
7. upon their Lord, the all-conquering who governs with all power, the merciful
8. God and father, all of them beseeching him with unrestrained cries and tears to frustrate the wicked design against them and rescue them by a wonderful
9. manifestation from the disaster imminently in store for them. So their prayer
10. went up fervently to heaven. Hermon drugged the pitiless elephants until they were filled with an abundant supply of wine and saturated with frankincense, and
11. in the early morning he appeared at the palace to inform the king. But that lovely gift of his creation, the interval of sleep, bestowed night and day since

the beginning of time by him who confers his blessings on whomsoever he chooses,

12. he sent upon the king. And the king, in the spell of the sweet, deep sleep God brought on him, was greatly thwarted in his lawless purpose and utterly disappointed in

13. his inflexible aim. The Jews, having escaped the appointed hour, praised their holy God and begged him who is quick to respond in mercy to show the power

14. of his mighty hand to the arrogant heathen. But the middle of the tenth hour had nearly arrived when the official in charge of the invitations noticed that the

15. guests were assembled and went to the king and shook him. He had trouble in awakening him, but then pointed out that the duration of the banquet was almost

16. past and reminded him of the circumstances. The king took account of what he said and then, turning to his cups, he ordered his guests at the banquet to take

17. their places opposite him. This done, he advised them to give themselves up to revelry, to appreciate the great honor conferred upon them and regard this late

18. part of the feast as all good cheer. After a period of table fellowship the king summoned Hermon and with severe threats inquired of him why the Jews had

19. been allowed to survive that day. But when he pointed out that he had carried out every last word of the king's bidding overnight and his friends confirmed it,

20. the king was seized with rage more fierce than Phalaris and said that the Jews had only sleep to thank for that day's grace. Then he added that the elephants should be prepared without delay for the coming day, in exactly the same fashion, for the extermination of the accursed Jews.

21. When the king had spoken, all who were present

readily assented together with
22. joy and each went off to his own home. But they used
the nighttime not so much for sleep as for devising all
sorts of insults for the people they thought were
23. doomed. The cock had no sooner crowed the dawn
than Hermon set the beasts
24. in all their paraphernalia in motion in the great colon-
nade. The crowds in the city thronged together for the
piteous spectacle, eagerly awaiting the first light of
25. morning. But the Jews, drawing their last brief breath
in tearful supplication and strains of lament,
stretched out their hands to heaven and implored the
Almighty
26. God once more to help them speedily. 1:9; 3:11; 4:16; 5:46
The rays of the sun were not yet widely dispersed and
the king was receiving his friends when Hermon presented himself and invited him to go forth, explain-
ing that his wishes were now ready to be
27. granted. When the king received his report he was
amazed at the outrageous invitation to go forth, overtaken as he was by complete ignorance, and asked
what business was on hand that required everything
to be completed for his sake with
28. such haste. But this was the working of the God who
governs all things who had
29. implanted in his mind forgetfulness of his previous
schemes. But Hermon and all his friends pointed to
the beasts and the troops and said, "Everything is in
30. readiness, King, in accordance with your firm purpose." However, he was filled with stern anger at the
words, since by the providence of God in this matter his
31. mind had gone blank, and gazing at him threatening-
ly, he said, "If your parents or your offspring were
here, I would have served them as an ample meal to
the wild beasts instead of the Jews, against whom I
have no complaint and who above
32. all others showed an absolutely unflinching loyalty to

my ancestors.
32. Indeed, if it were not for the affection that comes of
our habitual companionship and your
33. service, your life would have been taken instead of
theirs." So Hermon met with an unexpected and dan-
gerous threat and he cast his eyes down and his face
fell.
34. The king's friends, slipping out sulkily one by one,
sent away the gathered
35. throng, each to his own business. The Jews, on hearing what had happened with the king, praised the
God who had manifested himself, the Lord, the king
of kings, since they had obtained this help from him also.
36. Now the king once more arranged the whole
banquet in the same way and
37. ordered the company to turn to revelry. He then summoned Hermon and said menacingly, "How often,
wretch, must I give you orders on the self-same matters?
38. Fit out the elephants right now for tomorrow for the
extermination of the Jews."
39. But his kinsfolk who were at the table with him were
astonished at his
40. waywardness and remonstrated with him as follows:
"How long, King, will you make trial of us as though
we were fools? For the third time now you have
ordered us to exterminate the Jews, and once again
when the business is in hand you
41. change your mind and cancel your decree. All this
has put the city in a tumult of anticipation, and
already crowded with throngs of people, it has several times
42. now been in danger of being plundered." Thereupon
the king, a veritable Phalaris in every respect, was
filled with madness and, completely heedless of the
changes of heart which had been effected in him for
the protection of the Jews, vowed emphatically but

vainly that he would forthwith dispatch the Jews to the grave,
43. mangled by the knees and feet of the beasts, and that he would make an expedition against Judea and quickly level it to the ground with fire and sword and would swiftly burn down the Temple to which he had been refused admission and empty
44. it for all time of those who sacrificed there. Then his friends and kinsfolk left in great glee and high confidence and had troops posted in the most convenient spots in the city to keep guard.
45. The superintendent of the elephants drove the beasts almost, one might say, to the state of madness with fragrant draughts of wine mingled with frankincense and
46. equipped them with horrible implements. About dawn, when the city was already full of innumerable crowds making their way toward the hippodrome, he entered
47. the palace and incited the king to take up the business on hand. Then the king, his impious heart filled with stern anger, stormed out with the beasts, determined to watch without a qualm and with his very own eyes the spectacle of the
48. aforementioned Jews' painful and piteous destruction. When the Jews saw the dust stirred up by the elephants going out at the gate, the fully armed troops accompanying them and the movement of the people and heard the thunderous
49. din, thinking that the last crisis of their life and the end of their agonizing suspense had come, they took to wailing and moaning and kissed one another, embracing their relatives and falling on their necks, parents and children, mothers and daughters; some had newborn infants at their breasts, drawing their last milk.
50. Nevertheless, mindful of the former occasions on

which help was given from heaven; they threw themselves on their faces with one accord; they removed the
51. babes from breasts and cried out with an exceedingly great shout, imploring the ruler of all power by a manifestation to show mercy to them now that they were standing at the very gates of death.

Eleazar's prayer

1. **6** A certain Eleazar, a man of distinction among the priests of the country, already well advanced in years and a shining example of all life's virtues, directed the elders around him to stop calling on the holy God and prayed as follows: 2:1-20; 2Mac 6:18 4Mac 6:5; 7:1; LetArist 41
2. "King, great in power, Most High, All-conquering God, who governs the
3. whole creation with mercy, Pss 105, 106 look upon the seed of Abraham, upon the children of Jacob whom you sanctified, the people of your sanctified inheritance who are
4. perishing unjustly as strangers in a strange land. Pharaoh, the former ruler of this Egypt, with his multitude of chariots, high and mighty in his lawless insolence and boastful tongue, you destroyed in the depths of the sea with his proud host, Father, causing the light of your mercy to shine upon the people of Israel. Ex 15
5. Sennacherib, the cruel king of the Assyrians, exulting in his countless hosts, when he had subjugated the whole earth by the spear and was lifted up against your holy city, uttering grievous words with boastfulness and insolence, you shattered,
6. LORD, displaying your power openly to many nations. 2Kgs 19:35 The three comrades in Babylonia

who of their own choice gave their life to the fire
rather than serve idols you delivered unharmed to the
very hair of their head, making the fiery
7. furnace like dew, and you sent flame upon all their
enemies. Dan 3:27; PrAzar 25 When, through the slanderous accusations brought against him out of envy,
Daniel was thrown to the lions underground as food
for beasts, you brought him up to the light unscathed.
8. When Jonah was pining away unpitied in the belly of
the monster of the deep,
9. you, Father, restored him uninjured to all his household. Jonah 1:17-2:9 So now, you who hate insolence, full of mercy, protector of all, manifest yourself swiftly to those of the people of Israel who are
outrageously treated by the abominable and lawless
10. heathen. If our life is subject to penalty because of
impious deeds in the course of our sojourn abroad,
rescue us from the hand of our enemies, LORD, and
destroy
11. us by a fate of your own choosing. Let not those who
think vain thoughts bless their vain gods for the
destruction of your beloved people and say, 'Not
even their
12. God could rescue them.' WisSol 2:16-24; Ps 115:2 You who
possess all might and power, Eternal, look now upon
us. Pity us who are being put to death like traitors by
the mad insolence of
13. lawless men. Let the heathen fear your unconquerable power this day, highly
14. honored one, who are continually mighty to save the
people of Jacob. The whole
15. multitude of children and their parents implore you
with tears. Let it be made clear to all the nations that
you are with us, LORD, and have not turned your face
away from us, but even as you have said, 'Not even
when they were in the land of their enemies have I
neglected them,' so bring it to pass, LORD." Lev 26.44

A remarkable turnabout
in events and in the king's attitude

16. Just as Eleazar was finishing his prayer, the king arrived at the hippodrome
17. with the beasts and the whole wanton array of his army. And the Jews observed it and raised a great cry to heaven that made the surrounding valleys ring with the
18. sound and struck uncontrollable terror in all the hosts. Then the great and glorious, all-conquering and true God revealed his holy face and opened heaven's gates, from which descended two angels, clothed in glory and of awe-inspiring appearance,
19. visible to all except the Jews, 1En 14:20; TLevi 3:4
and they confronted the forces of their adversaries and filled them with confusion and timidity and bound them with immovable
20. fetters. The king also experienced a shuddering in his body and his gross insolence
21. faded to nothing. And the beasts turned back on the armed forces that followed
22. them and they began to trample them down and destroy them. The king's anger was now turned to pity and tears on account of the scheme he had previously
23. devised. For when he heard the outcry and saw them all prostrate to meet their
24. death, he wept and angrily threatened his friends, saying, "You usurp the king's power and excel tyrants in savagery, and you even attempt to deprive me myself, your benefactor, of my rule and indeed of my life, secretly devising measures that
25. are deleterious for my kingdom. Who has driven from their homes those who held the fortresses of our country with such loyalty and stupidly mustered them

26. here, each one? Who has so lawlessly surrounded
with torments those who from the beginning have in
every was exceeded all peoples in their goodwill
toward us
27. and have frequently submitted to the worst dangers
confronting men? Loose, yes loose completely their
unrighteous bonds. Send them back to their homes in
peace,
28. asking their forgiveness for what has been done to
them. Release the sons of the all-conquering, living
God of heaven, who from the times of our ancestors
until
29. now has conferred upon our estate an impregnable
stability with glory?" So the king spoke. The Jews
were released forthwith and blessed the holy God,
their savior, for their narrow escape from death.

The Jewish celebration of a feast of deliverance

30. Then the king left for the city and, summoning
the keeper of the public revenues, he ordered him to
supply the Jews with wine and all the perquisites for
a feast for seven days, decreeing that in the very
place where they had thought to meet
31. their fate they should hold a festival of deliverance
with all joy. Then those who had been reviled and
had just been close to the grave, or rather had already
had one foot in it, instead of a bitter and wretched
fate held a feast celebrating their deliverance, and
filled with gladness they portioned out to different
festive groups
32. the space that had been made ready for their destruction and burial. They left off the mournful sound of
dirges and took up the song of their fathers, praising
God the deliverer and worker of wonders, and laying
aside all wailing and lamentation, they formed

dances as a sign of the joy and peace that had come upon them.

33. The king likewise held a great banquet in celebration of all that had happened and endlessly returned solemn thanks to heaven for the unexpected deliverance granted

34. to him. But those who previously imagined that the Jews were doomed to destruction and to become a prey for the birds, and had joyfully conducted the registration, now groaned at being covered with confusion and at having their

35. blazing effrontery ignominiously quenched. The Jews, however, as we have said, having formed the dance just mentioned, spent the time in festivity, with glad

36. thanksgiving and psalms. And they laid down a general ordinance on these matters, to have effect wherever future generations might sojourn, that they should celebrate the aforementioned days with a festival of joy, not for the sake of drinking and gluttony but of the deliverance that had come to them through God.

37. They next petitioned the king, requesting him to dismiss them to their own homes.

38. Now the process of registration had gone on from the twenty-fifth day of Pachon to the fourth of Epiphi, for forty days, and the appointment of their

39. destruction from the fifth of Epiphi to the seventh, for three days. On these days the ruler of all revealed his mercy with great glory and rescued them one and all

40. unharmed. They feasted, with everything supplied by the king, until the fourteenth

41. day, when they made the petition for their dismissal. The king consented and on their behalf wrote the following letter to the generals in the cities, generously declaring his purpose.

The king's letter on behalf of the Jews

1. **7** "King Ptolemy Philopator to the generals in Egypt and all who have charge of
2. our affairs, greetings and good health; We, for our part, are in good health, and
3. our children also, the great God directing our estate as we desire. LetArist 37; 6:25-28 Some of our friends, out of malice, by urging the matter on us continually, persuaded us to gather the Jews together in the kingdom in a body and to inflict upon them
4. extraordinary punishments as traitors, suggesting that our state would never be stable because of the ill will the Jews bear to all nations until this was carried
5. out. So they brought them down with atrocious treatment, as slaves or rather conspirators, and they sought to put them to death without legal trial or even investigation, decking themselves out with cruelty more savage than the law
6. of the Scythians. But because of the fairness we show to all men, we reprimanded them for their conduct with stern threats and barely granted them their lives, and knowing of a surety that God in heaven protects the Jews, in alliance with them
7. continually like a father with his children, and taking account of their unshakable friendly disposition toward us and our ancestors, we have justly absolved them of
8. any blame whatever. And we have enjoined that all should return, each one to his own home, and that no one should do them any harm at all in any place or
9. reproach them for the unreasonable penalties inflicted on them. Be sure of this, that if we devise any evil scheme against them or cause them any trouble, we shall have not man but the most high God, who is

ruler of all power, as our adversary to exact vengeance for what is done, inexorably in all circumstances and for all time. Farewell."

10. On receiving this letter, the Jews did not at once make haste for their departure, but requested further of the king that those of the Jewish people who had wittingly transgressed against the holy God and his Law should receive the due punishment

11. at their hands, stressing that those who had transgressed the divine commandments for their belly's sake would never be well disposed to the king's business either.

12. The king acknowledged the truth of what they said, and praising them, he granted them full indemnity, to destroy without let or hindrance or any royal license or investigation those who had transgressed the Law of God anywhere in his dominion.

The Jew's joyous departure and return home.

13. Then, applauding him, as was fitting, their priests and the whole multitude

14. departed with joy, shouting the hallelujah. Any one of their countrymen they encountered on the way who had become defiled they punished and put to death

15. as a public example. On that day they put to death over three hundred men, and they

16. kept it as joyous festival, having subdued the unclean. But those who held fast to God even unto death enjoyed the full advantage of their deliverance and departed from the city crowned with all kinds of fragrant flowers, giving thanks to the God of their fathers, the everlasting savior of Israel, with gladness

17. and with shouting, in songs of praise and melodious hymns. When they had reached Ptolemais, called "rose-bearing" because of the special characteristic

of the place, the fleet waited for them, according to
their general wish, for seven
18. days, and there they held a banquet to celebrate their
deliverance, the king having generously supplied
every one of them with all they needed until their
arrival at
19. their own home. And when they had completed their
voyage in peace with appropriate thanksgivings,
there too in the same fashion as before they decided to
20. make these days also during the time of their sojourn
festival days. They consecrated them with an inscription on a pillar, and having dedicated a place of
prayer on the site of the banquet, they went away
unscathed, free, and filled with joy, and were conducted safely, by ordinance of the king, over land and
sea and
21. river, each to his own home. They had even greater
authority than before among their enemies and were
regarded with high esteem and awe; no one at all
extorted their
22. property. They recovered all their possessions,
according to the register, and those who had anything
of theirs returned it to them with great fear: The great
23. God had perfectly accomplished great things for
their salvation. 1:9, 16; 3:11; 4:16;
5:25; 7:22 Blessed be the deliverer of Israel forever and ever! Amen. 4Mac 18:24; Sir 51:30-38; Tob 14:15

PSALM 151

Translated from the Hebrew text
By J. A. Sanders

A Hallelujah of David the Son of Jesse.

1Smaller was I than my brothers
and the youngest of the sons of my father,
So he made me shepherd of his flock
and ruler over his kids.

2My hands have made an instrument
and my fingers a lyre;
And [so] have I rendered glory to the Lord,
thought I, within my soul.

3The mountains do not witness to him,
nor do the hills proclaim;
the trees have cherished my words
and the flock my works.

4For who can proclaim and who can bespeak
and who can recount the deeds of the Lord?
Everything has God seen,
everything has he heard and he has heeded.

5He sent his prophet to anoint me,
Samuel to make me great;
My brothers went out to meet him,
handsome of figure and appearance.

6Though they were tall of stature
and handsome by their hair,
The Lord God chose
them not.

[7]But he sent and took me from behind the flock
and anointed me with holy oil,
And he made me leader of his people
and ruler over the sons of his covenant.

In the line following the Hebrew text of this psalm another psalm (with its heading) begins, of which only two poorly preserved lines remain. Apparently they celebrate David's victory over Goliath; Sanders's translation is as follows:

At the beginning of David's power after
the prophet of God had anointed him.

[1]Then I [saw] a Philistine uttering
defiances from the r[anks of the Philistines].

It thus appears that the Greek text of Ps. 151 is a condensed recension of what was originally two separate psalms in Hebrew.

Translated from the Greek Text

This psalm is ascribed to David as his own composition (though it is outside the number[a]) after he had fought in single combat with Goliath.

I was small among my brothers,
and youngest in my father's house;
I tended my father's sheep.

[2]My hands made a harp,
my fingers fashioned a lyre.

[3]And who will declare it to my Lord?
The Lord himself; it is he who hears.[b]

[4]It was he who sent his messenger[c]
and took me from my father's sheep,
and anointed me with his anointing oil.

[5]My brothers were handsome and tall,
but the Lord was not pleased with them.

[6]I went out to meet the Philistine,[d]
and he cursed me by his idols.

[7]But I drew his own sword;
I beheaded him, and removed
reproach from the people of Israel.

[a] Other authorities add *of the one hundred fifty* (psalms)

[b] Some witnesses add *everything*; others add *me*; others read *who will hear me*

[c] Or *angel*

[d] Or *foreigner*

1: *Small . . . youngest,* 1 Sam. 16.7 and 11. *Tended . . . sheep,* 1 Sam. 16.11. One form of the Syriac version continues, "and I met a lion and also a wolf, and I killed them and tore them in pieces" (compare 1 Sam. 17.34-36). **2:** *My hands made a harp,* 2 Chr. 29.26. **4:** *Anointed me,* 1 Sam. 16.13; Ps. 89.20. *Took me from my father's sheep,* Ps. 78.70. **5:** *The Lord was not pleased with them,* 1 Sam. 16.7-10. **6:** *He cursed . . . by his idols,* 1 Sam. 17.43. Certain manuscripts of the Old Latin, Arabic, and Ethiopic versions continue, with minor deviations: "And I slung three stones at him in the middle of his forehead, and laid him low by the might of the Lord." According to 1 Sam. 17.49-50, David felled Goliath with only one stone. **7:** *His own sword,* 1 Sam. 17.51.

THE HOUSE OF THE MACCABEES (HASMONEANS)

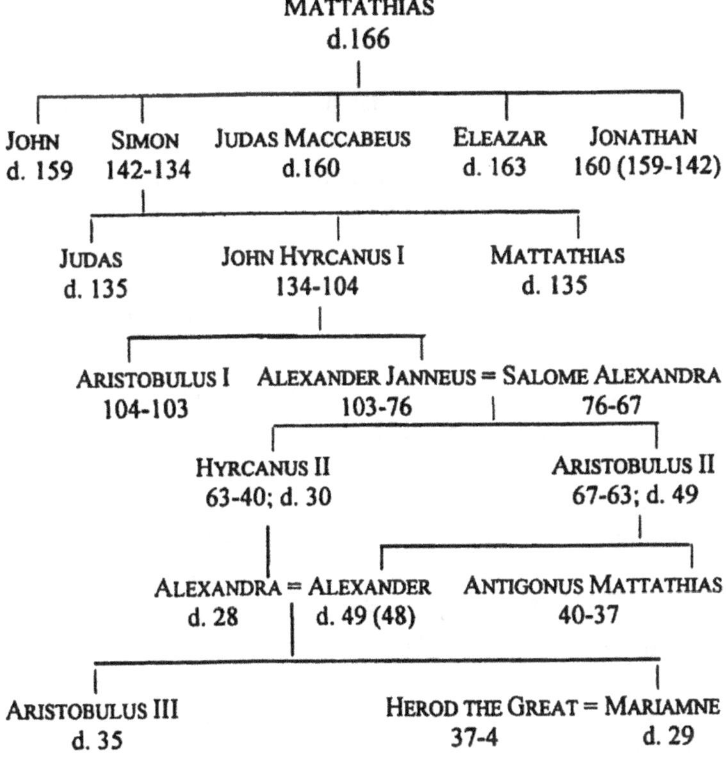

These two family trees include the names of the more important rulers. The presence of short parallel lines between two names indicate marriage. The date of an individual's death or the dates of his rule are in some cases disputed, and alternative possibilities are given within parentheses. All the dates are B.C. Besides the standard works on the chronology of the inter-testatmental period, special mention should be made of F. M. Heichelheim's "Chronological Table from 323-30 B.C." in *Proceedings of the IX International Congress of Papyrology*, Oslo, 1958, pp. 163-182 (also published separately by the Norwegian Universities Press). Seleucus I became king in the seventh year of the Seleucid era; see A. J. Sachs and D. J. Wiseman, "A Babylonian King List of the Hellenistic Period," *Iraq*, XVI (1954), p. 205. Syria became a Roman province in 64 B.C., and Pompey conquered Jerusalem in 63 B.C.

4 MACCABEES

(FIRST CENTURY A.D.)

A NEW TRANSLATION AND INTRODUCTION BY H. ANDERSON

The book widely known under the above heading is set in the form of a philosophical discourse in which the author proceeds to develop his argument by using the first person singular. In his preface in 1:1-6 he introduces the subject of his entire work, devout reason's mastery over the passions, a phrase which recurs like a refrain throughout (1:9, 13, 19, 30; 2:6, 24; 6:31; 7:16; 13:1; 16:1; 18:2). After intimating (1:7-12) that by far the best illustration of this proposition is the martyrdom of Eleazar and the seven sons and their mother, he moves into a philosophical and didactic section (1:13-3:18) in which he discusses the relationship of reason to the passions or emotions and furnishes examples from the lives of Old Testament heroes Joseph, Moses, Jacob, and David. There follows a brief historical exordium relating the intervention of Apollonius, governor of Syria, in the affairs of the Jerusalem Temple, its outcome, and the hostility of Antiochus Epiphanes to the Jews (3:19-14:26). So the scene is set for the martyrdoms to which the main body of the book is entirely devoted (5:1-17:6). Exceedingly detailed descriptions of the tortures to which all were subjected are interspersed with speeches from the lips of Eleazar and the sons, as well as with a panegyric on Eleazar in 6:31-7:23 and another on the sovereignty of devout reason in the seven brothers in 13:1-14:10. In 14:11-17:6 the mother is represented as, in her suffering and death, the most illustrious exemplar of the victory of reason, inasmuch as before her own end she exhorted her sons to endure death rather than transgress the Law. The final segment of the book is given to an account of the public effect of the martyrdoms (17:7-18:5) and of the mother's address to her children (18:6-19), and closes with an expression of faith in the justice of God and finally, a doxology (18:20-24).

Texts

The text of 4 Maccabees has been handed down in several manuscripts of the Septuagint, but most important are the Sinaiticus (S), from the fourth century A.D., and the Alexandrinus (A), from the fifth century. It does not appear in the third great uncial manuscript of the Greek Bible, the Vaticanus, but is found, with the exception of the section 5:11-12:1, in the eight- or ninth-century Codex Venetus (V). In addition, numerous manuscripts containing the works of the Jewish historian Josephus also contain 4 Maccabees, a fact which has, since the fourth century, led mistakenly, as we shall see, to the ascription of 4 Maccabees to Josephus. In any case, that 4 Maccabees was first issued without the name of the author is clearly indicated by its appearance in many manuscripts anonymously.

The Greek of our book (see Original Language) was early translated into Syriac, and it appears in the Peshitta under the title *The Fourth Book of the Maccabees and Their Mother,* a version which generally favors the reading of S against A. Some comparison of the Syriac with the Greek was undertaken in the joint work of R. L. Bensly and W. E. Barnes, published at Cambridge in 1895, titled *The Fourth Book of Maccabees and Kindred Documents in Syriac.*

The Fourth Book of Maccabees is not in the Vulgate and so is absent from the Apocrypha of the Roman Bible as well as from Protestant Bibles. However, Erasmus was responsible for a very free Latin paraphrase of 4 Maccabees, first published at

Cologne in 1524. He was not acquainted with the Greek text, which was in fact first printed in volume 3 of the Strasbourg Septuagint in 1526, but mav have worked from an old Latin version entitled Passio SS. *Machabaeorum*, somewhat closer to the Greek than Erasmus' rendering and extant in some thirty codices going back, probably, to an eighth-century archetype.

The first critical text of 4 Maccabees, founded, unlike the Strasbourg Septuagint of 1526, on a number of manuscripts, was that of O. F. Fritzsche, *Libri Apocryphi Veteris Testamenti Graeci* (Leipzig, 1871). H. B. Swete's edition, in volume 3 of *The Old Testament in Greek* (Cambridge, 1899), simply reproduces the text of A and furnishes variants from S and V. The text on which our translation is based is that of volume 1 of Rahlfs' *Septuaginta* (Stuttgart, 1935), which depends only on S and A. Our commentary draws attention only to those variants which significantly affect the sense of a passage.

The Fourth Book of Maccabees has a considerably stronger claim to the name "Maccabees" than 3 Maccabees, insofar as it witnesses events presumed to have taken place in the earliest days of the Maccabean revolt. Nevertheless, 4 Maccabees is in no sense a history of the exploits of the Maccabean leaders or of the course of the revolt. Rather, our author uses accounts of the martyrdoms as paradigmatic materials for a philosophical exercise on the subject of devout reason's mastery over the passions. Accordingly, even for 4 Maccabees, the designation "Maccabees" remains somewhat misleading. In the manuscript tradition different titles have been transmitted with the work, and the most appropriate and probably most original of these is the one cited by Eusebius and Jerome. On the Supremacy of Reason.

There is some question as to whether 4 Maccabees as we have it is the work of a single hand. Especially has the integrity of 18:6-19 been disputed, and several commentators consider the mother's speech to her children in these verses to be an interpolation. Their opinion is based chiefly on the supposed inferiority of style in the passage, on its catena of scriptural references, and on the discrepancy of its themes with reminder of the book. But there is no manuscript evidence for the omission of 18:6-19. Nor is there any strong reason to suppose that a rhetorician like the Jewish author of 4 Maccabees, intent on wedding Greek philosophy to Jewish religion, could not have rounded off his entire essay with an address of a rather more homespun type from his great heroine, celebrating the virtues of chastity and familial piety so dear to the Jews, elevating the heroes of the Jewish faith, and in short acting as the final spokeswoman for the supremacy of the Jewish religion. He could scarcely either have inserted the words attributed to the mother here at the close of her earlier speech in 16:16-23 without detracting from his focal point of interest, reason's sovereignty over the passions. So he allows the woman, whose own sovereign victory he has so lauded, to have the last word as the champion of Judaism. Consequently, we here treat the whole of 4 Maccabees as it stands in the Greek text as a unity.

Original Language

The chief aim of the writer of 4 Maccabees is to advocate fidelity to the Law and to demonstrate that the hope of fulfilling the Greek ideal of virtue resides only in obedience to the Law of Judaism. Accordingly, he is unquestionably a Jew. But he is no less certainly a Jew profoundly influenced by Greek philosophical thought and thoroughly at home with the Greek language. His work is conspicuously devoid of semitisms, and citations from the Old Testament consistently follow the Septuagint. The images, symbols, and metaphors employed as well as the antitheses, climaxes, and apostrophes that abound all clearly exhibit his skill in the craft of the Greek rhetorician. His Greek is free and idiomatic, indicating that the he thinks in that language; it is his native tongue. (9:19) These are but further indications of the writer's fluency in Greek and of the pervasive Greek atmosphere of 4 Maccabees.[1]

Authorship and date

Nowhere in 4 Maccabees is there any express notice given of its authorship, date, or place of origin. However, the work as a whole, as well as certain pieces of internal evidence, does allow us initially at least to make some reasonable, albeit broad and general, surmises on these matters:

1. We noted above that 4 Maccabees is found in a number of manuscripts containing the works of Flavius Josephus, the Jewish historian. Euisebius of Caesarea, in the early fourth century, and Jerome, a century later, attribute it to the hand of Josephus. But dismissing Ewald's suggestion[2] that another person by the name of Josephus may have been the author, we can also reject the traditional ascription of our book to the famous Flavius Josephus. Nowhere in his major works does the latter exhibit anything like the same florid rhetorical style as a 4 Maccabees - he is an historian where the writer of 4 Maccabees is primarily philosopher and rhetorician. Josephus reveals no acquaintance with the text of 2 Maccabees, which appear to lie behind 4 Maccabees. Nor is it at all likely that the eminent historian, who took the name of Flavius as a

compliment to the Flavian Caesar and married a gentile wife, would have championed the heroes of the resistance after the fashion of 4 Maccabees. Finally, to make but one specific point, whereas Josephus correctly describes Antiochus Epiphanies as the brother of Seleucus IV (*Ant* 12:4), in 4 Maccabees (4:15) he is called his son.

2. The manner in which the writer refers to the Jerusalem Temple and its services (e.g. 4:11f.) seems to presuppose that the Temple is still standing and therefore points to a date before the destruction of the Temple in A.D. 70. We may infer that the earliest possible date of composition is 63 B.C. The author is eager to explain that in the days of Seleucus IV (175 B.C.) the highest priest Onias held the office for life; this statement would have been unnecessary before 63 B.C., when life tenure lapsed after the fall of the Hasmonean dynasty.[3]

3. We can no longer think of Judaism in our period, even Palestinian Judaism, as distinct at all on most points from the cultural stream of Hellenism. Recent research has demonstrated ever more clearly that even in its homeland Judaism was influenced to hitherto unsuspected degree by hellenistic ideas, ideals, and practices.[4] However, traces of the infiltration of Hellenism into various phases of Palestinian Jewish life and thought are one thing, an almost complete absorption in hellenistic modes of conceptualization is another, and the ambiance of 4 Maccabees is so thoroughly and unreservedly Greek that to regard it as a product of Palestine is virtually impossible. The author's extensive knowledge of Greek philosophy, his positive and purposeful use of it to argue the supremacy of the Law, and his skill in Greek rhetoric undoubtedly point to a location beyond the boundaries

of Palestine, to a milieu in which East and West had completely met.

These arguments, limited as they are, do suggest that 4 Maccabees was written outside of Palestine by an unknown author in the period 63 B.C.-A.D. 70. Although we do not know the author's name, his work conjures up a vivid picture of the man - devotee of the Law of his people, theologian of considerable depth, philosopher and rhetorician in the Greek style, impassioned and imaginative narrator.

As to the date of 4 Maccabees, almost every generation between the time of Pompey (around 63 B.C.) and the Emperor Hadrian (around A.D. 120) has been proposed. In the Talmud, rabbinic accounts of martyrdoms, somewhat similar in form to the story related in 4 Maccabees, reflect the period of the persecution of Jews under Hadrian. Aside from the rather fragile evidence mentioned earlier that the Temple still appears to be standing, it is barely conceivable that, with its eloquent advocacy of the supremacy of the Jewish Law to the ethical systems of the pagan world and of the invincible power of Jewish faith and religion against all tyrannical attempts at suppression, 4 Maccabees could have been written after the Hadrianic persecution, when the Jews stood apart *contra mundum*, as it were. Accordingly, A. Dupont-Sommer assigns 4 Maccabees to the short period of relative quiet (A.D. 117-118) between the Jewish war at the close of Trajan's reign and the persecutions under his successor, Hadrian.[5] On the other hand, M. Hadas favors the reign of Caligula (A.D. 37-41), when the storm clouds of persecution were also gathering thickly. But is not necessary to look for an historical juncture when persecution or the imminent threat of it must have given rise to the considerations that appear in 4 Maccabees.[6] Definitive indications of the author's or readers', or hearers' situation vis-à-vis persecution or the absence of it are lacking from the work, and the theme of 4 Maccabees is not after all religious persecution as such. Rather does the writer offer a philosophical disquisition on the victorious strength of the devout reason, which would have been relevant and meaningful, at least to Jews of the Diaspora, almost anytime between Pompey and Hadrian, and for illustrative materials he draws upon what he clearly takes to be the classic martyrdoms under Antiochus Epiphanes in the early days of the Maccabean revolt.

In suggesting a date between A.D. 18 and 55, E. Bickermann follows a quite different line of argument and moves us on to rather firmer ground. There occur in 4 Maccabees words like *threskeia* = "religion" and *nomikos* (for the earlier *grammateus,* see 4Mac 5:4 and cf. 2Mac 6:18) = "expert in the law," which became fashionable only from the time of Augusta on. But more important, whereas 2 Maccabees speaks of Heliodorus, minister of Seleucus IV, as taking possession of the Temple treasures and describes him as *strategos* of Ceolesyria and Phoenicia (2Mac 3:5), 4Maccabees replaces this Heliodorus with Apollonius, governor of Syria and styles him *stretegos* of "Syria, Phoenicia, and Silicia" (4:2). This change can best be explained by assuming that an author like ours would naturally have employed the nomenclature obtaining under the conditions of the Roman imperial administration *in his own time*, when it appears that Syria and Silicia formed united parts of a single territory, and from Galatians 1:21, an inscription of A.D. 86, and a Roman agricultural writer by the name of Columella, it can be inferred that Syria-Silicia did in fact once constitute one province. Two passages in the *Annals* of the Roman historian Tacitus (2. 58; 13. 8) point to approximately A.D. 19-54 as the period during which Syria-Silicia make up one region for Roman administrative purposes, and Bickermann's view that 4 Maccabees falls somewhere within this period must be deemed a very plausible hypothesis.[7] But it is quite unjustified to go beyond this and maintain that, since there is no allusion at all to the persecution of Caligula, 4 Maccabees was written before the outbreaks of A.D. 38. As we have seen, reference, or the lack of it, to any particular persecution in a philosophical discourse like 4 Maccabees is a most unsure criterion of dating. Fortunately, the appreciation of such a philosophical work does not depend too largely on our ability to fix its immediate historical background precisely within the narrowest limits.

Provenance

Alexandria in Egypt has sprung naturally to the mind of a number of commentators as the likeliest place of composition. This city had an extremely large colony of Jews who were exposed constantly to the influence of Greek philosophy; it was also the city of Philo, with whose works 4 Maccabees has numerous points of contact. But the choice of Alexandria is based not so much on critical grounds or any specific indication of locality in 4 Maccabees itself as on a feeling for its general suitability. It may indeed tell against Alexandria that there is no reference to or quotation from 4 Maccabees in either Clement of Alexandria or Origin, and, in any case, as J. Freudenthal observed long ago, many Jewish hellenists composed their writings in widely disseminated parts of the Diaspora, far away from Alexandria; for example, Jason of Cyrene, Paul of Cilicia and Josephus himself.[8] Moreover, E. Norden, a leading expert in matters of Greek literature and language, found in 4 Maccabees an outstanding representative of that flowery, rhetorical "Asianic style" that was associated especially with Asia Minor and eventually blossomed to its fullest extent in the early second century A.D.[9]

If we look away from Egypt to the coastal lands of the northeast Mediterranean, the city that first suggest itself as a possible location for 4 Maccabees is Antioch in Syria, which was, according to Josephus, after Rome and Alexandria, the third city of the ancient world, where Greek rhetoric, and indeed all the arts, certainly did flourish, where there was also a large community of Jews, and where the early Christian movement established its first strong foothold on gentile soil. In later Christian tradition there are in fact certain indications of the existence of a cult of the Maccabean martyrs at Antioch. From the fourth century A.D., Jerome, for instance, testifies (somewhat ambiguously) to the veneration of the tomb of the Maccabees at Modein in Palestine, and is apparently thinking of the heroic leaders of the Maccabean revolt, but he seems to know also of physical relics of the martyrs (those described in 4Mac?) at Antioch. At approximately the same period at Antioch, John Chrysostom, in his *Fourth Homily*, conveys the impression of his preaching by the tomb of the martyrs, and later in the same work alludes to Eleazar and the mother and her seven sons, the very martyrs of 4 Maccabees.

Given the witness of these and other still later traditions to Antioch as the scene of a cult of the martyrs, there would seem to be no likelier home for 4 Maccabees, if we could also accept the view adopted by some recent interpreters, notably Dupont-Sommer and Hadas, that it was actually composed for oral delivery as an address of commemoration of the martyrs.[10] At this point the question of the place of origin of 4 Maccabees is intimately bound up with the question of its form. Our work has of course been variously characterized as a synagogue sermon, a lecture, a genuine commemorative address, or as a fictive discourse.

The main objection to regarding 4 Maccabees as a specimen of synagogue preaching[11] is that a synagogue sermon would almost certainly have been based on a text from scripture,[12] and although our knowledge of the homiletic practices of the synagogues of the Diaspora is very limited indeed, it is surely unlikely that even there a sermon would have begun in the highly philosophical vein of 4 Maccabees. By the same token, since as the work develops philosophical exposition gives way to fervent religious pleading, the classification of 4 Maccabees as a lecture[13] set within "the groves of academe" is no less improbable. We are thus left with two alternatives - a genuine commemorative address (delivered on the site of the martyrdoms at Antioch) or a literary piece of a rhetorical kind cast in the shape of a fictive discourse.

It has been maintained that 4 Maccabees was intended for oral delivery on a special occasion, and that the occasion was in fact the Jewish festival of Hanukkah. But the trouble with this assertion is, on the one hand, that, if composed for Hanukkah, 4 Maccabees must assuredly have alluded to the heroes of the Maccabean war whom that feast celebrates, which it never does, and, on the other hand, that there is no Jewish tradition that associates the martyrs of 4 Maccabees, Eleazar and the mother and her seven sons, with Hanukkah. It is with such considerations in mind that M. Hadas invites us to think of 4 Maccabees as a real address delivered at "an annual commemoration of the martyrs celebrated *at the site*, actual or supposed, of their burial."[14]

In support of this estimate of 4 Maccabees, appeal can be made to several passages which do seem to imply that it was spoken at the tomb of the martyrs on a day of special solemnity, especially 1:10, "I might indeed eulogize for their virtues those men who *at this season of the year* died together with their mother for goodness' sake," and 3:19, "But the season now summons us to expound the theme of the temperate reason" (although this latter may as well be translated, "But we have now reached the point in our discourse at which we are summoned to expound . . ."). Also, according to Dupont-Sommer,[15] the exclamation of 18:20, "Ah! bitter was the day and yet not bitter," evokes the particular day of commemoration of the martyrs, just as the mention of their tomb and epitaph in 17:8-10 suggests that the panegyric of 4 Maccabees was pronounced at the very site where they were buried.

However, only a pedantry quite foreign to the imaginative procedures of a rhetorician like our author would insist on the basis of 18:20 and 17:8-10 that he just *had* to be speaking on the day of commemoration at *the* actual tomb of the martyrs. None of the passages referred to in the foregoing paragraph are incompatible with the possibility of a set written piece, composed at a time of year traditionally associated with the death of the martyrs, in the form of a fictive discourse in which the author projects himself on to the rostrum, so to speak, in good rhetorical fashion, and confronts his readers directly. E. Norden draws attention to an essay in Cicero's Paradoxa in which he talks of "this speech," whereas he had already made it clear in the preface that he was *writing* late at night and was indeed choosing to do so in the form of direct speech.[16]

Besides, it may be asked whether the relatively wordy speeches placed on the lips of Eleazar, the sons, and, finally, the mother would have been natural in a spoken address. Again, if our author had delivered his panegyric at the very scene of the martyrdoms, by the tomb of the martyrs, would a rhetorician of his skill have lost the opportunity to make that movingly plain to his audience at 5:1 with words like "And so the tyrant Antiochus took his seat on this very spot where we are now gathered"? Instead he describes the location of the martyrdoms very vaguely indeed ("And so the tyrant Antiochus took his seat with his counselors on a certain high place" 5:1), so vaguely that the reader is given to think from what has gone before that Jerusalem may indeed be the setting for the martyr deaths. The possibility, therefore, that 4 Maccabees was in fact composed as a fictive discourse cannot be lightly dismissed.

Certain extrinsic factor also militate against the notion that 4 Maccabees was an address actually delivered on the site of the martyrs' burial. The Law expressly forbade contact with the dead (Lev 21:1-5, 10f.; Num 6:6-9; 19:11-13; Deut 18:9-12, 26:14), and the attitude of Jewish tradition toward anything resembling a cult of the dead is completely negative. Consequently, in order to regard 4 Maccabees as a commemorative speech at the martyrs' tomb in Antioch, we would have to think, as Hadas clearly recognizes,[17] of a thoroughly hellenized Jewish community in which hellenistic custom and usage in respect of the annual commemoration of heroes had altogether overcome natural Jewish reserve. Again, later Christian veneration of the Maccabean martyrs provides no guarantee of the existence of an earlier Jewish cult in the period of 4 Maccabees, with which the Christian commemoration stood in direct continuity.[18]

These consideration or reservations both about the form of our work and the actuality of a Jewish martyr cult in the first half of the first century A.D. considerably weaken the case for associating it with the tomb of the martyrs in Antioch. It may be best to follow E. Norden[19] in leaving the question of a home for 4 Maccabees much more open, contemplating only some possible location in the coastal lands of Asia Minor. Largely because of the numerous sea metaphors in the book, A. Kahana[20] conjectures one of the Aegean islands as a home for it, but the conjecture need not be taken too seriously, since almost anyone in the regions of the eastern Mediterranean could have indulged in sea metaphors, and, in any case, there are just as many metaphors of besieged cities, the land, and so on.

Historical Importance

The only complete Jewish work of its kind that has survived to us, 4 Maccabees is intrinsically of great historical value. Different in form and scope from anything that men of somewhat similar background and outlook, like Philo of Alexandria and Josephus, have given us, 4 Maccabees provides us with a particularly fascinating insight into the thought world of a hellenized Jew of the Diaspora in the first century of our era. Through 4 Maccabees we may appreciate his mastery of the Greek rhetorician's craft, his profound knowledge of Greek philosophical principles and his use of them to defend and illumine the sovereignty of the Law and the devout reason's control over the passions. But, as a source book of information on the external history of the writer's own time and place or of the early years of the Maccabean wars to which the martyrdoms he describes purport to belong, 4 Maccabees is of little value.

Our author, of course, is no historian. His aim is not to notify his reader as accurately as possible concerning long-past events of the Maccabean struggle. Rather does he seek, through all the rhetorical power he can muster, to let the stories he tells kindle the imagination of his readers, to move them to the depths in mind and heart, to persuade them to accept the supremacy of devout reason. The basic materials for his martyrdom stories were most probably derived from the tradition embedded in 2 Maccabees, although our author has patently stretched them and adorned them at will to suit his own philosophical and theological purposes, particularly in the speeches he has placed on the lips of the dying martyrs. Whether these stories have a foundation in genuine historical fact is an open question. If we have no means of proving their historicity, neither should we reject them out of hand as completely legendary. Perhaps a generation acquainted with the barbarities of Auschwitz and Buchenwald may be less prone to dismiss as terribly overdrawn and altogether fictional the bizarre and gruesome items in the repeated descriptions of the tortures in 4 Maccabees than the generation for which Townshend wrote in 1913, "The details of the successive tortures are elaborated in a way that shocks modern taste.[21]" Nevertheless, beyond reminding us that brave people almost certainly suffered severe torments and died as martyrs for the Jewish faith under Antiochus Epiphanes, 4 Maccabees adds nothing to our knowledge of the Maccabean period.

Theological importance

The writer of 4 Maccabees is a philosopher as well as a theologian. The framework of his thought is Greek, as are his mode of expression and the form of his work. He appears to have a firsthand intimacy with Platonic ideas, perhaps especially, as Hadas observes,[22] with Plato's *Gorgias,* in which Socrates concludes that the ultimate ideal or the true doctrine is to live and die in the practice alike of justice and of all other virtues. But he is closely acquainted also with the prevalent Stoic philosophy of his own day, and in many passages adopts Stoic language and echoes Stoic views (see e.g. 1:1, 6, 16f., 33; 2:7, 14; 3:11f.; 5:7-13, 19f., 22, 25, 38; 12:13; 13:19; 14:2; 15:4). However, his concern is not to advocate Stoicism or even to advance the knowledge of Greek thought among his readers, who are no doubt already "naturalized" in the Greek philosophical atmosphere. The philosopher in him never in fact overcomes the theologian, loyal to the faith of his fathers. All that he has learned from the Greeks is enlisted in the service of Judaism, to show that the cardinal virtues, self-control, courage, justice, and temperance, indeed the very essence of Greek wisdom, are subsumed under the Law or obedience to it.

Our author's religious priorities are nowhere more graphically illustrated than in the picture he presents of Eleazar in chapter 5. As the Jewish philosopher par excellence (5:4), Eleazar, far from endorsing Stoic principles, indeed opposes them, as when, for example, he insist against Stoicism that reason does not eradicate but only controls or directs the passions (5:23). Again, whereas Stoicism operated with the notion of the equality of sins, Eleazar follows Jewish tradition in distinguishing between light and serious sins (5:19-21).

But the real point at issue in Eleazar's confrontation with Antiochus, who is here spokesman for the Stoic viewpoint, is not the gradation of sins.[23] It is rather that the king is quite unable to comprehend what loyalty to the Jewish Law involves. The heart of Eleazar's doctrine is simply that "we must lead our lives in accordance with the divine Law" (5:15) and that "under no circumstances whatever do we ever deem it right to transgress the Law" (5:17). Accordingly, strict faithfulness to the law's command is the ground of his refusal to partake of swine's flesh or food sacrificed to idols. Antiochus, by contrast, brands this as a senseless scruple, engendered by a "preposterous philosophy" (5:11). For the king the act of eating swine's flesh is no more than the innocent enjoyment of one of nature's good gifts (5:9). For the old Jewish sage it is a matter of the utmost gravity since violation of any commandment, most of all violation in public in the presence of onlookers, constituted contempt for God the giver of the Law and was tantamount to apostasy (5:35-38).

Eleazar, who in 2 Maccabees is not at all recognized as a "philosopher," thus becomes the advocate of our author's own "philosophy" that the truth resides in the *eusebeia*, or piety, which inheres in obedience to the Law of Moses. His "philosophy" is in fact incapsulated in the rather strange and pregnant phrase *ho eusebes logismos* ("the devout reason," which enables the martyrs to master their natural feelings and desires throughout their fiery ordeal), which appears throughout the work as a recurring refrain and by which he invites not only his fellow Jews but the world at large to see that the sum of human wisdom and all the law of nature is gathered up under fidelity to the Law revealed by God to Israel.

The blend of particularism and universalism, implicit already in the term "the devout reason," accords well with our author's doctrine of God. For him the God who is first and foremost the God of the fathers of Israel (9:24; 12:18) is also the omniscient (1:12; 13:19) creator of the whole world (5:25; 11:5). He it is who fashioned man and implanted in him both his feelings and his reason (2:21f.). By his will alone personages like Antiochus are permitted to enjoy their regal status (12:11). He determines men's eternal destinies (18:5;cf. 12:19), recompensing the righteous martyrs and consigning the wicked to everlasting punishment. In all of this our author is in conformity with the Judaism of his day , and typically Jewish also is his appeal to biblical figures as archetypal models of the heroism of faith, Abraham (14:20; 16:20), Isaac (16:20, Jacob (2:19), Joseph (2:2), Moses (2:17), David (3:6), and Daniel and his companions (16:3, 21).

However, in one important respect, at least, our author's knowledge of Greek philosophy has positively affected his religious belief. Like Philo and the author of the Wisdom of Solomon, he subscribes to the idea of the immorality of the soul. The great hope expressed in 4 Maccabees is that the pure and immoral soul might enter into the incorruption of life everlasting (9:22; 14:5f.; 16:13; 17:12; 18:23). His espousal of the Greek doctrine of the immortality of the soul is clear-cut and striking; he consistently omits the passages in his primary source, 2 Maccabees, that testify unreservedly to the Jewish belief in the resurrection of the body (7:9, 11, 14, 22f.). Doctrinally, the most significant contribution of 4 Maccabees is the development of the notion that the suffering and death of the martyred righteous had redemptive efficacy for all Israel and secured God's grace and pardon for his people. Eleazar first expresses the idea in his prayer in 6:28f.: "Be merciful to your people and let our punishment be a satisfaction on their behalf. Make my blood their purification and take my life as a ransom for theirs." Later, we find the same thought: "The tyrant was punished and our land purified, since they became, as it were, a ransom for the sin of our nation. Through the blood of these righteous ones and through the propitiation of their death the divine providence rescued Israel, which had been shamefully treated" 17:21f.

The idea of vicarious atonement in and through the death of Jesus was of course of central importance in early Christianity, and it appears in many places in the New Testament (e.g. Mk 10:45; Mt 20:28; Heb 9:12; Rom 5; 1Tim 2:6; etc.). But there is no need whatever to suppose that passages like 6:28f. and 17:21f, in 4 Maccabees should be regarded as Christian interpolations. In fact, although the concept of vicarious atonement was by no means normative or widespread in Judaism around the time of Jesus or Paul, it does have roots going far back into the Old Testament and our author was certainly no innovator in this matter. One of the Levitical ordinances for the Day of Atonement is that the goat on which the lot for the Lord fell should be sacrificed and the blood brought into the holy place as a propitiation for the sins of Israel (Lev 16), since, as Lev 17:11 testifies, it is the blood that makes atonement. On a quite different level, the portrayal of the servant of Yahweh in Deutero-Isaiah bear witness to the saving effect for Israel of the suffering and sacrifice of an elect individual or group (see especially Isa 53:5, 10, 11). There is little doubt that the epic struggles of the Jews in the Maccabean wars gave further impetus to reflection not only on the positive value but on the atoning power of suffering and death. At any rate, the idea that the suffering and death of the righteous atoned vicariously for the sins of others is sufficiently well attested in the apocalyptic literature (e.g TBenj 3:8) and at Qumran (e.g. IQS 5:6; 8:3f., 10; 9:4) to suggest that it was in the air in the intertestamental period. Add to this its occurrence in less-developed form in 2 Maccabees 7:37f., and we can recognize that the readers of 4 Maccabees would certainly not have regarded the notion of vicarious redemption as a novel doctrine introduced by the author. Accordingly, when in its confessional formulations early Christianity laid great stress on the saving or redemptive efficacy of the death of Jesus, it was picking up and adapting to its own new faith a doctrine that already enjoyed at least a limited currency in Judaism.

Similarly, it is quite unnecessary to suppose that the notion of the Jewish martyrs being "received" after their death by Abraham, Isaac, and Jacob (4Mac 13:17) is an accommodation to the picture of Lazarus in the bosom of Abraham in Luke 16:22f. or that the idea of the partriachs and martyrs "living unto God" (4Mac 16:25) adumbrates a Christian view of the resurrection of the dead. Such ideas and images arise not by direct borrowing one way or the other between Judaism and primitive Christianity but rather from a common climate of thought and religious imagination shared by both.

In the last analysis our author's chief claim to fame rests not on any pioneering contribution he has made to a particular Jewish doctrine but on the fact that his work affords us a singularly valuable specimen of the way in which a hellenistic Jew of the Diaspora can draw upon Greek philosophical thoughts and modes of expression in the formation of an essentially religious message of enduring relevance and validity. The spur to withstand oppression and tyranny and to win spiritual victory over death itself is loyal obedience to the revealed will of God.

Relation to canonical books

Since our author's innovative genius lies "in his attempt to acclimate Judaism to a hellenized Diaspora, and thus prepare the way for making of it, and of its daughter religion, a universal faith,"[24] it is hardly surprising that his work shows no special indebtedness to any Old Testament book or books. If such men really did help to pave the way for the worldwide spread of Christianity, is there then any trace of the influence of 4 Maccabees on the New Testament? A. Deissmann, in fact, suggested that Paul may have been familiar with 4 Maccabees as a sort of current best seller, and he had in mind specifically the similarity between Paul's witness to the atoning death of Jesus and the testimony of 4 Maccabees to the vicarious atonement wrought through the deaths of the Jewish martyrs.[25] But a similarity in one point of doctrine between two authors is by means enough to justify a theory of direct borrowing one way or the other, and the most we should assume, as we have already indicated, is that Paul and our author, both hellenistic Jews of the Diaspora, were exposed to the same atmosphere of religious belief.

Relation to apocryphal books

The author of 2 Maccabees refers to his own work as an epitome of the five volumes of Jason of Cyrene. Few critics would deny that 2 and 4 Maccabees stand in some sort of relationship to each other. Both relate the martyr deaths of Eleazar and the mother and her seven sons, and both furnish an historical preamble to their accounts of the martyrdoms. However, whereas in 2 Maccabees the historical preamble is a lengthy and detailed report of the Syrian persecution and the martydroms are briefly told in less than two chapters (6:18-7:41), in 4 Maccabees the historical preamble (3:20-4:26) reads like a short resume of 2 Maccabees, and the martyrdoms, described in the most elaborate detail, occupy fourteen chapters (5-18).

Freudenthal argued that the phenomena presented by the two texts, the similarities and discrepancies between them, are best accounted for by supposing that each author used Jason's history as a basic source and selected and adapted from it what best suited his own intention and design.[26] Heliodorus, mentioned thirteen times in 2 Maccabees, completely disappears from 4 Maccabees and is apparently replaced by Apollonius (4Mac 4:2). This must be due to confusion about the identity of the person referred to by the many pronouns employed in the Jason source. The longer form of the speech of the dying Eleazar in 4 Maccabees 6:26-29 (cf. the short form in 2 Mac 6:30) is to be taken as a faithful transcript of the text of Jason. Similarly, while 2 Maccabees 7:41 merely notes quite simply that "after the sons the mother died," 4 Maccabees 17:1 describes her as committing suicide by throwing herself on the flames. This is a piece of information derived from Jason but suppressed by the author of 2 Maccabees because he repudiated suicide as evil. Such is the gist of Freudenthal's argumentation.

The case for 4 Maccabees' use of Jason is not at all convincing.[27] Nothing whatever of Jason's work has survived, and, given the literary devices of the day, it is possible that the claim of the author of 2 Maccabees to be Jason's epitomist is only a fictional piece of propaganda to lend authority to his writing. Freudenthal's thesis that 4 Maccabees depends on Jason's history is unconvincing; it requires us to make of our author much more of a factual reporter fastidious about accurate reproduction of his source than from his work he really appears to be. In this regard Dupont-Sommer's remark is very much to the point: "The history of temperate reason is certainly more than mere history."[28] The writer of 4 Maccabees' main aim was to move his reader deeply by the pathos of his story, and he was first and foremost a rhetorician of skill and inventiveness and not a recorder of facts. A man like this knew above all how to develop, enlarge, and embellish a story to produce the desired effect upon his readers. If he had at hand the data provided by 2 Maccabees, he certainly did not need a fuller source like Jason's history for the many, many additions he has made to the narrative of the martydoms. His own imagination, aided and abetted perhaps by developments of the tale within ongoing oral tradition, would have been quite enough to do the trick. In all likelihood then our author had at his disposal 2 Maccabees and rearranged and reshaped it freely to suit his own taste and purpose. The relative dates of the two works and the obvious parallels in sequence as well as in content, as the list in Townshend[29] clearly demonstrates, offer additional support for this view.

There are certain rather close resemblances in religious thought and outlook between 4 Maccabees and the Wisdom of Solomon: belief in the incorruptibility and immortality of the soul, the everlasting life of the righteous as a life of communion with God (WisSol 3:9 ; cf. 4Mac 7:19; 9:8; 16:25;

17:18), the notion emanating from Neo-Pythagorean astralism of the immortal souls of the martyrs shining bright like the stars in heaven (WisSol 3:7; cf. 4Mac 17:5). Freudenthal thought that the author of the 4 Maccabees not only knew the Wisdom of Solomon but that he had it before him when he wrote. In his view the long passage in 4 Maccabees 5:23f. is a deliberate extension or elaboration of the simple statement in the Wisdom of Solomon 8:7; "The fruits of wisdom's labor are virtues, for she teaches self-control and understanding, righteousness, and courage; and there is nothing in life for men more profitable than these."[30] But there is little or no verbal similarity between the two passages, and in both we are dealing with common Stoic arguments. We can infer no more from the parallel thought of the two passages than that both writers were familiar with Stoic ideas. From other parallels in thought between the two documents (e.g. the immortality of the soul) it is impossible to adduce proof of direct literary connection or dependence of 4 Maccabees on the Wisdom of Solomon. All we are entitled to say is that the authors shared a similar background of religious ideas.

Cultural importance

In 4 Maccabees, as in 2 Maccabees, the story of the martyrdoms is set in the early days of the Maccabean revolt and the persecutor is Antiochus Epiphanes. No traces of 4 Maccabees are discernible, however, in later Jewish tradition, where the story circulated in a wide variety of forms for many centuries. In the rabbinic literature the martyrdoms are assigned to the Hadrianic persecution (see LamR 1:16; b.Git 57b; PR 43:180; SER 30:151), and in some rabbinic accounts the name of the mother, not given in 4 Maccabees or in 2

Maccabees, is Mariam bat Tanhum. In Syriac Christian accounts she is called Shamone and/or Maryam, whereas a Spanish reviser of the *Sefer Josippon* (c. A.D. 953; edited at Constantinople in 1510) named her Hannah, no doubt under the inspiration of the story of Hannah in 1 Samuel 1f., and especially 1 Samuel 2:5 (Hannah's prayer: "The barren woman bears sevenfold, but the mother of many is desolate").

Representations of the martydoms in works of art (e.g. the macabre pictures of the fourteenth and fifteenth centuries), poetry, and drama down to modern times are probably dependent on later versions of the story stemming from traditions independent of 4 Maccabees (or 2Mac). The same may be true also of such early iconographic depictions of the martyrdom of the Maccabees as on the Brescia Casket (c. A.D.370).

It is unquestionably in the sphere of Christian martyrology that 4 Maccabees specifically exerted the most profound and widespread influence, most of all among early Church Fathers both of the East and West, like Gregory Nazianzus and John Chrysostom. Ambrose, and Augustine. They not only knew and used 4 Maccabees but almost adopted it as a "Christian" book insofar as they looked upon the Jewish martyrs as Christian protomartyrs. In his oration on the martyrs, Gregory, for instance, refers to the first of August as the annual day of their commemoration and holds them up as worthy of universal honor, with the reminder (alluding to Heb 11:40) that none of those who were made perfect before Christ reached that point outside of the Christian faith. Indeed, later on in his work he commends them for having lived according to the cross even though they lived before it.[31] Likewise Chrysostom, author of four homilies on the Maccabean martyrs, vividly portrays Christ as the one who draws the aged mother into the contest of the arena of torment. Augustine, for his part, notes clearly (*City of God* 18:36) that it was "on account of the extreme and wonderful suffering of the martyrs told therein" that the books of the Maccabees were taken over and preserved by the Church. Ambrose's *De Jacob et vita beata* is hardly more than a transcript of our book.

Further testimony to the influence of 4 Maccabees in Christian circles is borne by the *Passio ss. Machabaeorum*, a free Latin adaptation of our work belonging possibly to the fourth century A.D. This was probably the Latin text freely paraphrased by Erasmus in his edition of 4 Maccabees, first published at Cologne in 1524 and dedicated to his friend Elias Maraeus, president of the "most honorable college of Maccabees at Cologne." Erasmus was evidently familiar with a shrine of the Maccabean martyrs at Colgne, where Maccabean relics were greatly revered. According to tradition, relics of the martyrs had been transported from Antioch, the place of their burial, to Byzantium by St. Helen, later from Byzantium to Milan by Eustorgius, and finally from Milan to Cologne in 1164 by Reginald, bishop of that city.

Erasmus' interest in 4 Maccabees was assuredly not simply academic. He began his paraphrase in 1517, the very year when Luther nailed his pamphlet against indulgences to the door of the church at Wittenberg. And some six years later the works of the great humanist were submitted to the Spanish Inquisition. No wonder he suffered his own dread of martyrdom. To be sure, he found in the message of 4 Maccabees stimulus, uplift, and encouragement. Erasmus' appeal to 4 Maccabees sums up within itself what has been the supreme cultural importance of the work - not only has it provided materials for the literary and theoretical development of Christian martyrology which became a matter of prominent concern in the religion of Europe, but its "martyr-saints" have been a model and an inspiration to fortitude and perseverance for many under the heel of tyranny and persecution.

THE FOURTH BOOK OF MACCABEES

The author's definition of his task

1 1 Highly philosophical is the subject I propose to dis-
cuss, namely, wether devout reason is absolute master of the passions,[a] and I would strictly counsel you
to
2 give earnest attention to my philosophical exposition.[b] The subject is an indispensible branch of
knowledge but it also includes a eulogy of the greatest of
3 virtues,[c] by which I mean of course prudence. If reason is shown to be master
4 of the passions that hinder temperance, namely gluttony and lust, it is also demonstrated that it is lord of
the passions that impede justice, such as malice, and
over the passions that impede courage, such as rage
and fear and pain.[d]
5 How then, some might ask, if reason is master of the
passions, does it not control 2:24
6 forgetfulness and ignorance? The question is absurd.
It is not over its own inherent defects that reason is
master but over the passions that are opposed to justice and courage and temperance, and master over
these not in such a way as to eradicate them but to
keep men from surrendering to them.[e]
7 I could prove to you from many and varied
sources that reason is absolute
8 master of the passions, but far the best example I
could furnish is the heroism of those who died for
virtue's sake, namely Eleazar and the seven brothers
and
9 their mother.[f]

Taking no account at all of the sufferings that brought them to
10. their death, they all proved that reason is lord of the passions. I might indeed eulogize for their virtues those men who at this season of the year[g] died together with their mother for goodness sake, but I would rather congratulate them on the
11. distinctions they have attained. Not only was all mankind stirred to wonder by their courage and fortitude, but even their own torturers, and so they became responsible for the downfall of the tyranny which beset our nation, overcoming the tyrant by their fortitude so that through them their own land was purified.[h]
12. But I shall have opportunity presently to speak on this matter. Meanwhile, I shall begin, as I am accustom to do, with the general theory, and then I shall turn to their story, giving glory[i] to God the all wise.

The supremacy of reason

13. The subject of discussion then is whether reason is absolute master of the passions.
14. But we have to define what reason is and what passion is, how many forms
15. of passion there are, and whether reason is lord over them all. Reason, I suggest
16. is the mind making a deliberate choice of the life of wisdom. Wisdom, I submit
17. is knowledge of things divine and human, and of their causes.[j] , And this wisdom, I assume, is the culture we acquire from the Law, through which we learn the
18. things of God reverently and the things of men to our worldly advantage.

19 The forms of wisdom consist of prudence, justice, courage, and temperance. Of all these prudence is that most authoritative, for it is through it that reason controls the
20 passions. Of the passions, the two all-embracing kinds are pleasure and pain,
21 and each of these inheres in the body as well as the soul. A large retinue of
22 passions attends upon both pleasure and pain. Before pleasure comes desire, and
23 after pleasure comes joy. Before pain comes fear, and after pain comes sorrow,
24 Anger is a passion involving both pleasure and pain, if one reflects on how it
25 has touched him.[k] Included under pleasure also is the malicious moral temper
26 which expresses itself in the most widely varied ways of all the passions, those of the soul being pretentiousness and avarice and seeking the limelight and
27 contentiousness and backbiting, those of the body being a voracious appetite for
28 all kinds of food[l] and gluttony and gormandizing in private. Now pleasure and pain being, as it were, two branches stemming from body and soul, there are
29 many offshoots of these passions.[m] Each of these reason, the master gardener, purges thoroughly and prunes and binds up and waters and irrigates all around[n]
30 and so domesticates the wild undergrowth of inclinations and passion.[o] For reason is the guide of the virtues and the supreme master of the passions.
31 Observe in the first place how, in regard to the things that hinder temperance, reason is complete

master of the passions. Temperance, as I understand it, is
32 control over desires, and of desires some relate to the soul and others to the
33 body, over both of which reason obviously holds sway. When we are attracted to forbidden foods, how to we come to reject the pleasures to be gained from them? Is it not because reason has the power to control the appetites? I believe
34 it is. Accordingly, when we crave seafood or fowl or the meat of four-legged beasts or any sort of food at all that is forbidden to us under the Law, it is through the
35 mastery of reason that we abstain. For the proclivities of our appetites are restrained and held in check by the prudent mind, and all the motions of the body are muzzled by reason.

The Law's compatibility with reason

1 2 What wonder, then, if the desires of the soul for union with beauty are deprived
2 of their force? It is on these very grounds that the temperate Joseph is praised, because through his own rational faculty he gained mastery over his sensuality.
3 Though a young man at the prime of his sexual desire, he quenched the burning
4 ardor of his passion. Gen 39:7-12

And not only the fiery passion of sexual desire does
5 reason evidently exercise control, but over all desire. For the Law says, *You*
6 *shall not covet your neighbor's wife or anything that is your neighbor's.* Ex 20:17

Surely then, since the law tells us not to covet, I should the much more readily persuade you that reason has the power to control the desires.
7 It has the power, indeed, over the passions which hinder justice. For how else could a man who habitually gormandizes in private or is gluttonous or a drunkard be taught to change his ways if reason were not obviously lord over the passions?
8 As soon as a man conducts himself according to the Law, then even if he be avaricious, he reverses his own natural tendency and lends to the needy without
9 interest, canceling the debt with the coming of seven-year periods.[a] And if a man be niggardly, he is brought under the rule of the Law through reason, so that he neither gleans over the stubble in his harvest fields nor picks the last grapes from his vines.

Det15:9;23:20;Ex22:24; Lev 25:36-53

And in other cases also we can perceive that reason is master of the passions.
10 For the Law[b] takes precedence over benevolence to parents and will not betray
11 virtue for their sake: it takes precedence over love for a wife and reproves her
12 for transgression; it overrules love for children and punishes them for wrongdoing; and
13 it exercises its authority over intimate relationships with friends and rebukes
14 them for evil. Nor should you think it paradoxical that reason is able through the Law to master enmity so that a man will not cut down the trees in his enemy's orchard and will save the property of his adversary from marauders and raise up his beast when it has fallen.[c]

Duet 20:19; Ex 23:4f

15 Reason is also obviously in control of the more
aggressive passions, ambition,
16 vanity, false pretension, pride, and backbiting. All
these malicious passions the temperate mind rejects,
as it does even with anger, since over it too it has the
17 mastery. When Moses grew angry with Dathan and
Abiram, instead of venting
18 his anger upon them he moderated it by reason.[d]
Num 16:23-30
For the temperate mind, as I have said, has the
power to triumph over the passions, to transform some of
them
19 and quell others. How else did our surpassingly wise
father Jacob blame Simeon and Levi and their
friends for slaughtering the whole tribe of the
Shechemites
20 without any appeal to reason, and declare, *Accursed
be their rage?* Gen. 34
Surely if
21 reason could not control anger, he would not have
spoken in this way. When Gen 49;7
22 God fashioned man, he implanted in him his
passions and inclinations, and at the same time,
enthroned the intellect amid the senses as the sacred
guide over
23 all. To the intellect he gave the Law, and if a man
lives his life by the Law he shall reign over a
kingdom that is temperate and just and good and brave.

Reason's conquest of the passions, as in King David

24 How is it then, someone may object, that if
reason is master over the passions, it does not
control forgetfulness and ignorance? 1:5

1 3 The argument is absolutely ludicrous, for reason is clearly not sovereign over
2 its own inherent inclinations but over those of the body.[a] For instance, none of you can eradicate desire, but reason can ensure that you do not become enslaved
3 to desire. Anger none of you can eradicate from his soul, but reason can help
4 you resist anger. None of you can eradicate malice, but reason may be your ally
5 in not allowing you to be overwhelmed by malice. For reason is not the uprooter of the passions but their antagonist.
6 This becomes even clearer, in fact, when we consider the case of King David's
7 thirst.[b] When David had been fighting against the Philistines throughout the entire day and in company with the soldiers of his own people had killed many of them, 2Sam 23:13-17; 1Chr 11:15-19
8 with the evening he came to the royal tent all perspiring and very tired, and
9 around it was encamped the whole army of our ancestors. While all the rest took
10 to dining, the king, parched with thirst as he was and though he had plentiful
11 springs of water, was unable to slake his thirst for them. An unreasonable desire for the water in the enemy's territory racked him and inflamed him and
12 unnerved him and burned him up. When his bodyguard grumbled at the king's desire, two stalwart young soldiers who respected it equipped themselves fully
13 with armor and, taking a pitcher, scaled the enemy's ramparts. Escaping the notice of the sentries at the

gates, whey went through the whole enemy encampment
14 on the search. On finding the spring, the boldly drew from it an carried the
15 drink to the king. But he, though still burning with thirst, considered that a drink reckoned as equivalent of blood presented a dreadful danger to his soul.
16 Accordingly, he set reason against desire.and poured out the drink as a libation
17 to God. For the temperate mind is able to conquer the constraints of the passions
18 and quench the flames of frenzied desire, to overcome the pains of the body,[c] however extreme, and through the nobility of reason to reject contemptuously the whole domination of the passions.

The divine punishment of Apollonius, governor of Syria, in the Temple.

19 But the season[d] now summons us to expound the theme of the temperate reason.
20 When our fathers were enjoying profound peace through their observance of the Law and were faring so well that even the king of Asia, Seleucus Nicanor,[e] set
21 moneys aside for their Temple service and recognized their polity,[f] just then certain men took repressive measures against the communal harmony and implicated us in various disasters. EX 30:12; 2Chr 24:6
1 **4** A certain Simon set himself up as political opponent of Onias, a man of highest integrity, who was then high priest and held the office for life,[a] but when, in spite of spreading all sorts of slander, he failed to harm him in the eyes of the

2 people, he went off into exile with a view to
betraying his country. He then made his way to
Apollonius, governor of Syria, Phoenicia, and
Silicia, and said,
3 "Sympathetic as I am to the king's interest, I am
here to inform you that thousands upon thousands of
private deposits are store in the treasury at Jerusalem
in which the Temple holds no share, and so they
rightly belong to King
4. Seleucus." 2Mac 3:7-34
Apollonius, having checked out the details of the
matter, praised Simon for protecting the king's
interest and went up to Seleucus and disclosed
5 the fact of these large funds. Armed with full
authority to deal with the business, he proceeded
quickly to our country with the accursed Simon and
a very powerful
6 army.[b] He declared he had come at the king's
command to take over the private
7 deposits in the treasury. Our people complained and
protested at the announcement, reckoning that it was
outrageous for those who had entrusted their
deposits to the Temple treasury to be deprived of
them, and they did all they could to prevent
8.9 him. But Apollonius, with threats, made his way to
the Temple. Then the priests and the women and
children made supplication to God in the Temple to defend
10 his holy place, which was being desecrated. and
when Apollonius, with his armed soldiery, marched
up to seize the moneys, angels on horseback
appeared from
11 heaven with flashing armor[c] and filed them with fear
and trembling. At that Apollonius fell down half
dead in the court of the gentiles, and he stretched out

his hands to heaven and with tears entreated the Hebrews to pray for him and
12 propitiate the heavenly host. He had so sinned, he said, as to merit death, but if only he were spared he would sing before all men praises to the blessedness of the
13 holy place. Moved by these words, despite his anxiety[d] lest King Seleucus should think that Apollonius was overthrown by human design and not by divine
14 justice, Onias the high priest prayed for him. And after his miraculous deliverance, Apollonius went off to reveal to the king what had happened to him.

Antiochus' savage measure against the Jews

15 One the death of King Seleucus, his son[e] Antiochus Epiphanes, an arrogant and
16 terrible man, succeeded to the rule. He deposed Onias from the high priesthood and
17 appointed his brother Jason as high priest on his agreeing to pay him annually three thousand, six hundred, and sixty talents[f] if he would confer the office on 2mac 4:8-10
18 him. So Antiochus commissioned Jason to serve as high priest and rule over the
19 people. In total disregard for the Law, Jason changed the nation's whole mode
20 of life and its polity; not only did he lay out a gymnasium on the citadel[g] of our 2mac 4:12
21 native land but he also rescinded the service of the Temple. At his the divine
22 justice was angered and brought Antiochus himself to war

against them. When he was at war with Ptolemy in Egypt[h] and heard
that the people of Jerusalem took the greatest delight in a widespread rumor about his death, he promptly marched
23 against them. And when he had ravaged them he issued a decree to the effect that
24 all who were seen to conform to their ancestral Law must die. And when by his decrees he failed completely to destroy our people's respect for the Law,
25 and observed that all his threats and penalties were entirely discounted, even to the extent that women who knew in advance what was in store for them were hurled headlong from the walls with their infants because they had their children
26 circumcised; when, I say, his decrees were despised by the people, he himself sought to force each individual in the nation under torture to partake of unclean food and to abjure Judaism.[i]

Antiochus' encounter with Eleazar

1 **5** And so the tyrant Antiochus took his seat with his counselors on a certain high
2 place,[a] with his fully armed troops mustered around him, and he ordered his guards to drag along every single one of the Hebrews and compel them to eat
3 swine's flesh and food sacrificed to idols. Whoever refused to eat the defiled
4 food was to be tortured and put to death. Many were violently snatched away and the first of the herd to be brought before Antiochus was a man called Eleazar, of priestly stock, expert in the Law and advanced in age, and known to many of the

5 tyrant's entourage for his philosophy,[b] 2Mac 6:18-31*
When Antiochus saw him, he said,[c]
6 "Before I have the tortures begun on you, old man, I would advise you to eat
7 of the swine's flesh and save yourself. I respect your age and your gray hairs, although to have had them for so long and still cling to the religion of the Jews
8 makes you anything but a philosopher in my eyes. Why should you abhor eating
9 the excellent meat of this animal which nature has freely bestowed on us? Surely it is sheer fully not to enjoy harmless pleasures, and it is wrong to spurn nature's
10 good gifts. But in my judgment it will be greater folly still if you indulge in idle
11 conceits about truth and continue to defy me to your own cost in suffering. Will you not awaken from your preposterous philosophy, abandon your nonsensical calculations, assume a frame of mind to match your years, and accept the true
12 philosophy of expediency? Bow to my benevolent advice and have pity on your
13 own old age. Consider this also, that, even if there is some power that watches over this religion of yours, it would pardon you for any transgression committed under compulsion."[d]
14 When the tyrant had in this way urged him on to the eating of food forbidden
15 by the Law, Eleazar asked permission to speak, and on receiving authority to do
16 so he began to speak out publicly as follows: "We, Antiochus, who firmly believe that we must lead our lives in accordance with the divine Law, consider that no compulsion laid on us is mighty enough to overcome our willing

17 obedience to the Law. Therefore, under no circumstances whatever do we ever
18 deem it right to transgress the Law. And even if our Law was not, as you suggest, in truth divine, and we only reckoned it to be divine, it would still in fact be
19 impossible for us to ruin our reputation for piety.[e] Accordingly, you must not
20 regard it as a minor sin for us to eat unclean food; minor sins are just as weighty
21.22 as great sins, for in each case the Law is despised.[f] You mock at our philosophy
23 as though our living under it were contrary to reason. On the other hand, it teaches us temperance so that we are in control of all our pleasures and desires; and it gives us a through training in courage so that we willingly endure all
24 hardship; and it teaches us justice so that whatever our different attitudes may be we retrain a sense of balance; and it instructs us in piety so that we most highly
25 reverence the only living God. Therefore, we do not eat unclean food. Believing that God established the Law, we know that the creator of the world, in giving
26 us the Law, conforms it to our nature.[g] He has commanded us to eat whatever will be well suited to our souls, and has forbidden us to eat food that is the
Lev 11:1-23
27 reverse. It is the act of a tyrant to compel us not only to transgress the Law but also to eat, so that you may laugh at us for partaking of the unclean food that is
28.29 abhorrent to us. But you will not have your laugh at my expense. I will not violate the solemn oaths of my ancestors to keep the Law, not even if you gouge
30 out my eyes and burn my entrails. I am neither so old nor short of manliness
31 that in the matter of religion my reason should lose its youthful vigor. So set the
32 torturer's wheel turning and fan the fire to a great

blaze. I am not so sorry
33 for my old age as to become responsible for breaking
the Law of my fathers.
34 I will not play you false, O Law my teacher, I will not
forswear you, beloved self-
35 control; I will not shame you, philosophic reason, nor
will I deny you, venerable
36 priesthood and knowledge of the Law. You shall not
defile the reverent lips of
37 my old age nor my lifelong service of the Law. Pure
shall my fathers welcome Gen 15:15
38 me,[i] fearless of your punishments even unto death.
Tyrannize as you will over the ungodly, but you will
never lord it over my thought on the subject of true
religion, neither by your words nor through your
works."[j]

Eleazar's amazing bravery under torture

1 **6** After Eleazar responded so eloquently to the
tyrant's exhortations, then the
2 guards who stood around dragged him roughly to the
implements of torture. First they stripped off the old
man's clothes, though he was still adorned with the
3 beauty of his piety. Then, binding his arms on either
side, they scourged him
4 with whips, while right up against him a herald
shouted, "Obey the king's
5 command!" But the great-souled and noble man, a
true Eleazar,[a] refused absolutely
6 to recant as if the torture were no more than a dream,
and, keeping his eyes raised aloft to heaven, the old
man let his flesh be torn by the scourges until his
7 blood ran freely and his sides were lacerated. He fell
to the ground when his body could no longer endure
the pain, but his reason he kept erect[b] and inflexible.
8 With his foot one of the merciless guards kicked

him savagely on the side to
9 make him get up as he fell. But he suffered the torment and scorned the
10 compulsion and overcame the pains, and under a hail
of blows, the old man, like
11 a true athlete, prevailed over his torturers. His face
beaded with sweat and panting heavily, he roused his
very torturers to amazement at his fortitude.
12 13 Thereupon, partly out of pity for his old age,
partly in sympathy through previous friendship, partly in admiration of his courage, some of the king's
14 courtiers went up to him and said, Why, Eleazar, are
you so unreasonably
15 destroying yourself in this foul way? Let us bring
you some of the cooked food, and you pretend to
taste of the swine's flesh and save yourself."[c] 2Mac 6:21

16 But as if their counsel only made his wounds all
the harder to bear, Eleazar
17 cried aloud, "Never may the children of Abraham
think such evil thoughts as
18 out of cowardice to enact a part so ill-becoming to
us.[d] It would most surely be contrary to reason if,
having lived our lives in accordance with the truth
right up to our age and having preserved our fair reputation for so living in conformity
19 with the Law, we should now change and ourselves
become a model of impiety
20 to the young by setting them an example of eating
unclean food. Shameful would it be if we should,
with only a very short space of life left to us,[e] become
a
21 laughingstock in the eyes of all for our cowardice
and be despised by the tyrant
22 as craven because we would not champion our
divine Law to the death. Therefore,
23 O children of Abraham, you must die nobly for

piety's sake. And you, guards of the tyrant, why
leave off your work?"
24 When they saw him so high in spirit in the face
of such constraints and so
25 adamant against their offer of mercy, they brought
him to the fire. There they burned him with cun-
ningly devised instruments and threw him in the fire
and
26 poured an evil-smelling concoction into his nostrils.
And when his flesh had been burned away to the very
bones, and he was on the point of expiring, he lifted
his
27 eyes to God and said.[f] "You know, O God, that
though I could have saved
28 myself I am dying in these fiery torments for the sake
of the Law. Be merciful
29 to your people and let our punishment be a satisfaction on their behalf.
30 Make my blood their purification and take my life as
a ransom for theirs."[g] With these words the holy man
nobly succumbed to his torments and by his reason
held his ground through the very tortures of death for
the Law's sake. 1:11; 6:28; 9:24; 12:18; 17:20-22; 18:4
31 32 Confessedly then, devout reason is master of the
passions. For if the passions were sovereign over
reason, I would have credited them with testimony to
their
33 superiority. But since we have just shown how reason conquers the passions, we
34 properly confer upon it the authority of leadership. It
is only right that we should confess reason's sovereignty insofar as it rules over torments inflicted on us
from
35 outside ourselves - it would be absurd to do otherwise.[h] The arguments I adduce demonstrate wisdom's actual sovereignty not only over pains but its
rule over pleasures and its complete refusal to yield

A panegyric on Eleazar

1 **7** Like an outstanding pilot, indeed, the reason of
our father Eleazar, steering the
2 vessel of piety on the sea of passions, though buffeted by the threats of the tyrant
3 and swamped by the swelling waves of torture, in no
way swerved the rudder of
4 piety until he sailed into the haven of deathless victory. No city beleaguered by many devices of all
kinds has ever offered such resistance as did that perfect saint. When his sacred soul was assailed with
blazing rack and torture, through reason,
5 the shield of his piety, he overcame his besiegers.
Stretching out his mind like a protruding cliff, our
father Eleazer shattered the wild surges of his passions.
6 O priest worthy of your priestly office, you did not
defile your sacred teeth, nor did you pollute with
unclean food a stomach that had room only for piety
and
7 purity. O mind in perfect unison with the Law, and
philosopher of the divine
8 life! So must all those be who are skilled in the craft
of keeping the Law and who defend it with their own
blood and noble sweat even in the face of sufferings
9 unto death. You, father, by endurance that brought
you to glory,[a] have confirmed our adherence to the
Law, and your august speech on holiness you have
not annulled, but through your deeds you have rati-
fied your words of divine philosophy.
10 O aged man, mightier than torture; revered elder
more vigorous than the flame;
11 great king, ruler of the passions, Eleazar! Even as
our father Aaron, armed with the censer, ran through

our father Aaron, armed with the censer, ran through
the massed company of his people and overcame the
fiery
12 angel, so did Aaron's descendant Eleazar not deviate
in his reason, though
13 consumed in the fire.[b] Num 17:1-15; WisSol 18:20-25 But most
wonderful of all, though he was an old man, and the
sinews of his body were already unstrung, his mus-
cles all relaxed and his
14 nerves weakened, by means of reason be became
youthful again in spirit and by
15 reason like Isaac's prevailed over many-headed torture. Gen 22 O blessed old age, revered gray head, life
level to the Law and perfected by the faithful seal of
death.
16 If, therefore, an old man despised torments unto
the death on account of his
17 piety, we must admit that devout reason is leader
over the passions. But some may contend that not all
men are masters of the passions, because not all men
18 possess enlightened reason. Only those who with all
their heart make piety their
19 first concern are able to conquer the passions of the
flesh, believing that to God they do not die, as our
patriarchs Abraham, Isaac, and Jacob died not, but
live to
20 God.[c] Mk 12:26; Rom 6:10; 14:8; Gal 2:19, 16:25 Accordingly, the
validity of our argument is not impaired by the fact
that some men seem to be ruled by their passions
because of the weakness of their
21 reason. For what philosopher is there, who lives by
the whole rule for philosophy
22 and believes in God and knows that it is blessed to
endure every pain for the
23 sake of virtue, who could fail to master his passions
for the sake of piety? Only the wise and courageous
man is ruler of the passions.

The King's invitation to the seven brothers to recant their ancestral faith

1 **8** Yes, indeed, even young lads have become
philosophers through devout reason
2 and have triumphed over still more severe torments.
For when the tyrant had been so conspicuously foiled
in his first attempt, having been unable to compel the
old man to eat unclean food, then in violent rage he
ordered others of the Hebrew captives to be brought
and said that if they would eat of the unclean food
they would be released, but if they refused, they
would be even more savagely
3 tortured. When the tyrant had issued these commands, seven brothers in the company of their aged
mother were brought before him, handsome and
modest and
4 well-born and altogether charming. On seeing them
standing around their mother in the midst, as though
they were a chorus, the tyrant was struck by them,
and astounded at their comeliness and nobility, he
smiled at them and called them
5 near and said, "Young men, I admire you each and
every one and ant to show you favor, and since I
greatly respect the beauty of such a large band of
brothers, I not only advise you not to display the
same mad frenzy as that old man who has just been
tortured, but I beg of you to yield to me and take
advantage of my
6 friendship. Just as I am able to punish those who disobey my orders, so am I
7 able to benefit those who obey me. Take my word
for it then that if you will renounce the ancestral law
of your polity you will receive leading positions of
8 authority over my domains. Share in the Greek style,

9 living, and enjoy your youth.[a] If you provoke me to
anger by your disobedience, you will compel me to
the use of dreadful punishments to destroy each and
every
10 one of you by torture. Have pity on yourselves, for
though I am your enemy, I
11 myself feel compassion for you in your youth and
beauty. Will you not reflect that if you disobey there
is nothing in store for you but death with torments?"
12 With these words he ordered the instruments of
torture to be brought forward
13 in order to terrorize them into eating of the unclean
food. The guards then brought forward the wheels
and joint dislocators, racks and wooden horses, catapults and cauldrons, braziers and thumbscrews, iron
claw and wedges and bellows,[b] and
14 the tyrant spoke up again and said, You must be
afraid, my lads, and the justice you revere[c] will be
merciful to you if you transgress under duress."
15 But they, when they heard his enticing words and
saw the fearful machines of torture, not only were
not frightened but even resisted the tyrant with their
own
16 philosophy, and by their right reasoning brought
down his tyranny. Just think, however, what sort of
arguments they would have used if some among
them had
17 been fainthearted and cowardly. Would they not
have gone like this? "What wretched and extremely
foolish creatures we are that, when the king invites
us
18 and presses us to accept his benevolence, we should
not consent! Why do we sport such vain resolutions
and venture a disobedience that will be the death of
19 us? Shall we not, my brothers, fear these instruments
of torture, take account of
20 the threats of torment, and abandon this vainglory

and fatal bragging? Let us
21 take pity on our own youth and have compassion for
our mother's old age, and
22 let us lay it to heart that if we disobey we die. The
divine justice will pardon us.
23 for being afraid of the king under duress. Why
should we remove ourselves from
24 this most pleasant life and deprive ourselves of this
sweet world? Let us not
25 resist necessity nor vaunt ourselves to our own cost
in torture. Not even the Law itself would willingly
condemn us to death for being afraid of the instruments of
26 torture.[d] Why should we be so absorbed in contentiousness or so attracted to an obstinacy that must
prove fatal when we could obey the king and live an
untroubled
27 life? But on the very point of being tortured these
young men uttered no such
28 words nor even entertained such thoughts. For they
despised the emotions and
29 were masters over pain. Accordingly, no sooner had
the tyrant finished counseling them to eat unclean
food than they all with one voice and as with one
soul said:[e]

1 **9** "Why do you delay, tyrant? We are prepared to
die rather than transgress the
2 commandments of our forefathers. We should truly
bring shame upon our ancestors if we did not live in
obedience to the Law and take Moses as our
3 counselor. Tyrant, who counsel us to transgress, do
not in your hatred of us pity
4 us more than we pity ourselves. We reckon that your
clemency which offers us deliverance in return for
our transgression is harder to bear than death itself.

5 You seek to terrify us with your threat of death by
torture as if you had learned 5:4-6:30
6 nothing from Eleazar but a short while ago. But if,
for the sake of their religion and enduring through
torments, old men of the Hebrews have remained
faithful to the end, if is even more appropriate that
we who are young should die in disregard of the tortures you impose on us, the very tortures our aged
teacher
7 triumphed over. Put us to the test then, tyrant; and if
you take our lives for the
8 sake of our religion, do not think you can harm us
with your torments. By our suffering and endurance
we shall obtain the prize of virtue and shall be with
God,
9 on whose account we suffer. But you, because of our
foul murder, will suffer at the hand of divine justice
the everlasting torment by fire you deserve."

The torture and defiance of the first and second sons

10 Indignant at these words expressing the youths'
disobedience, the tyrant was even
11 more enraged at their ingratitude. Then, at the word
of command, the guards brought forward the eldest
brother, ripped off his tunic, and bound his hands and
12 arms on either side with thongs. But when they had
flogged him with whips and for all their strenuous
effort had made no impression on him, they cast him
on
13 the wheel. When he was racked on it, the limbs of
the noble youth were put out
14 of joint, and as limb after limb was broken,[c] he
denounced the tyrant and said,
15 "Most abominable tyrant, enemy of heaven's justice
and bent on slaughter, you punish me in this fashion

and bent on slaughter, you punish me in this fashion
not as a murderer or man of impiety but as a champion
16 of the divine Law. "The guards then said to him,
"Consent to eat and so save
17 yourself from the tortures." But he replied, "Your
wheel is not so strong, base underlings, as to strangle
my reason. Sever my limbs, burn my flesh, twist my
18 joints, and through all these torments I will prove to
you that the children of the
19 Hebrews alone are invincible in the defense of
virtue" When he said this they
20 spread fire under him and fed the blaze, drawing the
wheel still tighter. The wheel was besmeared all over
with his blood, and the heap of coals was quenched
by the discharge fluid dropping down, and bits of
flesh whirled around on the
21 axles of the machine. Even when his bodily frame
was all dissevered, the great-
22 souled youth, a true son of Abraham, uttered not a
groan. As though he were being transformed into
incorruption by the fire,[d] he nobly endured the torments Mal 3:2
23 and said, "Imitate me, my brothers; do not become
deserters in my trial nor
24 forswear our brotherhood in nobility. Fight the
sacred and noble fight for true religion and through it
may the just providence that protected our fathers
become
25 merciful to our people and take vengeance on the
accursed tyrant." With these words the saintly youth
expired.
26 While they all marveled at his bravery of soul,
the guards brought forward the brother next to him in
age, and when they had adjusted the sharp-clawed
iron

27 hands, they fastened him to the torture machine and
the catapult. On inquiring of him whether he was
willing to eat before the torture began, they heard his
28 noble resolve, and then proceeded to tear at his
sinews with the iron hands and ripped off all the flesh
from his cheeks and the skin of his head, like wild
29 leopards. This agony he endured with courage and
said, "How sweet is every kind of death for the sake
of our ancestral religion." And to the tyrant he said,
30 "Does it not occur to you, most bloodthirsty of
tyrants, that you are being tortured more than I, when
you see that the arrogant reasoning that belongs to
your tyranny
31 is overcome by our endurance for true religion's
sake? I am sustained in my ordeal by the joys that
arise from defending virtue, but you are tortured by
the
32 threats that confront impiety. You cannot, vile tyrant,
escape the penalties of the divine wrath."

The torture and defiance of the third and fourth sons

1 **10** When he had barely met his illustrious death, the
third son was brought forward amid fervent exhortations from many people to taste of the food and save
2 himself. But he cried aloud and said, "Do you not
know that the very same father begot both me and
my brothers, and the same mother bore us all, and
3 I was brought up on the same doctrines? I do not
abjure the noble bond of
4 brotherhood. Therefore, if you have any means of
torture, apply it to my body,
5 for my soul you cannot touch even if you would"[a] At
the man's outspoken pronouncement they were
grievously annoyed, and with their dislocating
machines they dislocated his hands and feet, and by

the use of levers they sundered his
6 limbs from their sockets; and they twisted his fingers and arms and legs and
7 elbows. And when they could by no means strangle (his spirit), they abandoned their machines and with the tips of their fingers[b] they scalped him as the Scythians
8 do. Then they brought him at once to the wheel, and on it his backbone was disjointed until he saw bits of his flesh in shreds and gluts of blood pouring from
9.10 his entrails. On the point of death he said, "We, vile tyrant, suffer all this for
11 our training in divine virtue. But for your impiety and savagery you will suffer endless torments."
12 When he had died in a manner worthy of his brothers, they dragged forward
13 the fourth one and said, "Do not you, too, display the same madness as your
14 brothers, but obey the king and save yourself." But he replied, "For me you
15 cannot heat the fire so hot as to make a coward of me. By the blessed death of my brothers, by the everlasting ruin of the tyrant, by the glorious life of the pious,
16 I will not deny our noble brotherhood. Contrive whatever torture you will, tyrant, that you might go on learning from them that I am brother to those
17 who have been tortured already." On hearing this the bloodthirsty and murderous and
18 altogether abominable Antiochus ordered his tongue to be cut out. But he said, "Even if you remove the organ of speech, God still hears those who are silent.
Isa 53:7-12
19 Look, my tongue is hanging out; cut if off, for you will not thereby make my
20 reason mute. Gladly, for the sake of God, do we allow the limbs of our body to

21 be mutilated. But you God will speedily overtake,
since you are cutting out the tongue that sang songs
of praise to him." Isa 35:6

The torture and defiance of the four remaining sons

1 **11** When he, too, who had been so cruelly afflicted
with tortures died, the fifth
2 son sprang forward and said, "I waste no time in
demanding the torture for
3 virtue's sake, but of my own accord come forward so
that you might kill me and for your further misdeeds
incur the punishment the heavenly justice will inflict on
4 you. You enemy of virtue and enemy of man, what
have we done that you
5 destroy us in this way? Is it because we revere the
creator of all and live according
6.9 to his virtuous Law? But such conduct deserves
honors, not torments.[a] While he spoke these words
the guards bound him and dragged him to the catapult.
10 They bound him to it by his knees, and fastening
them to it with iron cramps, they twisted his loins
back over the circular wedge untill he was curled
back on
11 the wheel like a scorpion and his limbs were all disjointed.[b] And thus, struggling
12 for breath and racked in body, he said, "A glorious
favor you bestow on us, tyrant, thought all unwilling,
enabling us as you are to manifest our constancy
toward the Law by yet more noble sufferings."
13 When he had died, the sixth son was brought forward - a mere lad. The tyrant
14 then asked if he was willing to eat and be released.
But he replied, "I am younger

15 in age than my brothers, but just as old in reason. We
were born and reared for the same purpose, and we
are likewise obliged to die in the same cause.
16 Accordingly, if you want to torture me for not eating
unclean food, do your
17.18 torturing now," When he said this they brought
him to the wheel, and stretching him out on it carefully until his backbone was disjointed, they set the
fire going
19 under him. And heating up sharp skewers, they ran
them into his back, and
20 piercing his sides, they burned out his entrails. But
under all this torment he declared, "How sacred and
seemly is the agony to which so many of my brothers and I have been summoned as to a contest in sufferings for piety's sake, and yet
21 we have not been vanquished. For religious knowledge, tyrant, is unconquerable.
22.23 Fully armed with goodness I, too, shall die along
with my brothers, and I myself, too, shall confront
you with one great avenger more,[c] you deviser of new
24 tortures, you enemy of men of true religion. Six of
us, lads though we are, have
25 destroyed your tyranny. For your inability to sway
our reason or to force us to
26 eat unclean food, is not that your ruin? Your fire is
cool for us and your catapults
27 painless and your violence powerless. No tyrant's
guards, but the guardians of the divine Law have
been our protectors, and that is why our reason
remains undefeated."

1 **12** When he, too, had died a blessed death, having-
been cast into the cauldron,
2 the seventh and youngest son of all came forward.
Moved with pity toward him, even though he had
been fiercely exasperated by his brothers, and seeing

the bonds already placed on him, the tyrant asked
him to come closer and attempted
3 to persuade him, saying, "You see the outcome of
your brothers' folly; they
4 have been duly punished for their disobedience and
are dead. And you, too, if you refuse to obey, will be
miserably tortured and will yourself meet a premature
5 death. But if you do obey you will be my friend and
will be given charge over
6 my affairs of state." While he thus appealed to him,
he sent for the boy's mother so that he might show
pity of her over the loss of so many sons and further urge
7 on the sole surviving son the obedience that would
save him. But when the mother gave encouragement
to her son in the Hebrew tongue, as we shall shortly
8 relate,[a] "Loose me," he said, "and let me speak to the
king and all the friends
9 who are with him." 2Mac 7:22-40
And in great glee over the boy's promise, they quickly
10 11 loosed him. Then he ran to the nearest brazier and
said, "Impious man, of all the wicked ones you most
ungodly tyrant, are you not ashamed to receive your
kingdom with all its blessings from the hand of God
and then to kill those who
12 serve him and torture those who practice piety? In
return for this, justice will hold you in store for a
fiercer and an everlasting fire and for torment which will
13 never let you go for all time. Are not you, who are
but a man, ashamed, you savage beast, to cut out the
tongues of men who share the same feelings as you
and are made of the same elements[b] and to torture
them in this brutal fashion?
14 They, for their part, have died nobly and so fulfilled
their piety toward God, but you will groan dreadfully
for having slain the champions of virtue without cause."
15.16 Then when he, too, was on the point of death, he
declared, "I shall not prove

17 deserter to my brothers' valor. I call upon the God of
my fathers to be merciful
18.19 to our people. You he will punish both in the present life and in death." With this prayer against the
tyrant, he threw himself into the braziers and so gave
up his life.[c]

A panegyric: reason's sovereignty in the seven sons

1 **13** Now, therefore, if the seven brothers scorned
sufferings even unto death, it must be universally
conceded that the pious reason is complete master of
the passions.
2 For if being enslaved to the passions they had eaten
unclean food, we
3 would have said that they had been conquered by
them. However, in this case it did not happen so, but
by the reason which is commended by God they prevailed
4 over the passions, and so we cannot but perceive the
mind's supremacy over
5 them since they overcame both passion and sufferings. How then can we fail to admit, in regard to
these men, right reason's victory over the passions,
seeing that
6 they did not shrink from the pains for fire?[a] Even as
towers at the entrance to harbors repulse the threatening onslaughts of the waves and provide a calm
haven
7 for those who sail into it, so the seven-towered right
reason of the youths fortified
8 the haven of piety and tamed the rugged license of
the passions. They formed a
9 holy choir of piety as they encouraged each other
with the words. "Let us die like brothers all, broth-

ers, for the Law's sake, Let us follow the example of
the three youths in Assyria, who despised the same
trial by ordeal in the furnace.[b] Dan 3
10 11 Let us not be pusillanimous in the demonstration
of true piety." Courage,
12 brother!" said one, and another, "Hold on nobly!"
And another, recalling the past, said, "Remember
whence you came and at the hand of what father
Isaac Gen 22
13 gave himself to be sacrificed for piety's sake." Each
one severally and altogether, looking at each other
with most cheerful mien, aglow with courage, said,
"With all our hearts let us consecrate ourselves unto
God, who gave us our
14 souls, and let us expend our bodies for the custodi-
anship of the Law. Let us have
15 no fear of him who thinks he kills. "Great is the
ordeal and peril of the soul that lies in wait in eternal
torment for those who transgress the commandment
of God. Matt 10:28
16 Let us then arm ourselves with the control over the
passions which comes from
17 divine reason. After our death in this fashion
Abraham and Isaac and Jacob will
18 receive us, and all our forefathers will praise us."
And to each one of the brothers as they were dragged
away, those who were left said, "Do not shame us,
brother, nor be traitor to our brothers who have
already died."
19 You cannot be ignorant of the charm of brotherhood which the divine and all-wise providence has
allotted through fathers to their offspring, implanting
it, in
20 fact, in their mother's womb. There brothers dwell
for the same period and are formed over the same
duration of time; they are nurtured from the same
blood

21 and are brought to maturity through the same source
of life. They are brought to birth through same span
and draw milk from the same fountains, and through
22 being embraced at the same breast, fraternal souls are
nourished, and they grow from strength to strength
through a common nurture and daily companionship
as
23 well as in the training imposed by our discipline in
the Law.[a] The ties of brotherly love, it is clear, are
firmly set and never more firmly than among the
seven
24 brothers; for having been trained in the same Law
and having disciplined themselves in the same
virtues, and having been reared together in the life of
25 righteousness, they loved one another all the more.
Their common zeal for beauty and goodness straight-
ened their goodwill and fellow feeling for one another,
26 and in conjunction with their piety made their brotherly love more ardent.
27 Nevertheless, although with them nature and companionship and high moral character added to the
charms of brotherhood, it was through their piety that
the surviving sons had the endurance to look upon
their brothers while they were being racked with pain
and tortured to death.

1 **14** More than that, they even urged them on to face
the torment, and so they not only despised the sufferings but also mastered the strong feelings of brotherly love.
2,3 O reason, more kingly than kings, more free than
freeman! How holy and
4 harmonious the concord of the seven brothers for
piety's sake! Not one of the
5 seven lads turned coward, nor cowered away from
death, but all, as though

6 running on the highway to immortality, hurried on to
death by torture. Just as hands and feet move in unison with the prompting of the soul, so did those holy
youths, as if impelled by the deathless soul of piety,
go in harmony to the death
7 for piety's sake. O all-holy sevenfold assembly of
brothers in harmony! For just
8 as the seven days of creation move around piety, so
did the youths in chorus circle
9 around the sevenfold assembly, dissolving the terror
of torture.[a] Even now we shudder when we hear of
the affliction of those young men; but they, not only
looking on with their own eyes, not only hearing the
instant threat pronounced against them, but actually
suffering the torment, endured to the end, and that in
10 the agonies of burning - and what could be more
painful than these? Sharp and immediate is the
power of fire and quickly did it destroy their bodies.

The mother in her death the most shining example of the victory of reason

11 Do not count it amazing that in those men reason
triumphed over tortures,[b]
12 when even a woman's mind scorned still more manifold torments; for the mother of the seven youths
endured the agonies inflicted on every one of her
children.
13 Consider how tangled is the web of a mother's love
for her children so that her
14 whole feeling is the profoundest inward affection for
them. Even animals not possessed of reason have an
affection and love for their young similar to that of
15 human beings. Among the winged creature the tame

ones shield their young by
16 nesting under the roofs of houses,[c] while those that
build their nests on the peaks of mountains and in the
clefts of rocks and in the holes or tops of trees hatch
their
17 young and ward off the intruder. But if they cannot
ward him off they flutter around about the nestling in
the pangs,of love and call to them in their own
18 speech and assist their offspring in whatever way
they can. But what need is
19 there to demonstrate the affection of irrational animals for their young when even the bees fend off
intruders at the season of making the honeycomb and
pierce with their sting like a sword those who molest
their young and defend them to
20 the death? But not even her affection for her young
caused the mother of the youths, whose souls was
like Abraham's,[d] to waver.

1 **15** O reason that was lord over the passions of the
sons![a] O piety that was dearer
2 to the mother than her sons! When two options lay
before her, namely piety or
3 the instant deliverance of her seven sons according to
the tyrant's promise. she
4 loved piety better, which preserves to eternal life
according to God's word. How can I possibly
express the deep love of parents for their children?
On the tender nature of the child we impress a wonderful likeness of soul and form,[b] and especially
mothers, who are more affectionate in their own feelings toward their
5 children than fathers. For mothers are weaker in
their being than fathers, and the
6 more children they bear, so much the more do they
love their children. But no mother ever loved her

children more than the mother of the seven sons, who in
7 seven childbirth's implanted in herself a profound affection for them; and because of the many pains she suffered in each case was constrained to feel her bond of
8 love with them; but on account of her fear of God she discounted the immediate
9 safety of her children. Indeed, because of her sons' moral heroism and their
10 willing obedience to the Law, she cherished an even greater love for them. For they were just, and temperate, and brave, and magnanimous, and so filled with love for each other and for their mother that in obedience they kept the Law even
11 unto death. Nevertheless, although all the many promptings of maternal love pulled the mother toward the bond of affection for them, in not a single case did
12 their varied tortures avail to sway her reason, but each and every child and all
13 of them together did the mother urge on to death for piety's sake. O sacred nature, parental love, filial affection,[c] nurture, and unconquerable maternal
14 affections. Each one she saw racked and burned, yet for piety's sake remained
15 unwavering. She saw the flesh of her children melt away in the fire and their toes and fingers scattered on the ground, and the flesh of their heads right down
16 to the cheeks laid out before her like masks. O mother, sorely tired now by pains
17 sharper than the pains of birth! O woman who alone among women brought
18 perfect piety to birth! Your firstborn, as he breathed his last, did not sway your resolve, nor the second, as he looked on you with pity in his torment, nor the
19 third, as he expired; nor when you beheld the eyes of

each one immovably fixed on the same anguish amid
the tortures, nor indeed when you observed in their
20 nostrils the signs of approaching death did you break
into tears. When you saw your children's flesh
burned on children's flesh, and severed hand upon
hand, and flayed head upon head, and corpse fallen
upon corpse, and when you saw the place crowded
with spectators of your children's torments, you did
not weep.
21 Not the sirens' melodies nor the sweet sound of the
swan's song so charm the hearers ears as do the children's voices charm their mother when they speak to
22 her from amid the tortures. With what a manifold
host of torments then was the
23 mother tortured while her sons were racked by the
wheel and fire. But in the midst of her passionate
feelings pious reason nerved her whole being with a
manly courage and enabled her to transcend the
immediate affections of a mother's love.
24 And although she saw the destruction of her seven
children and the endlessly varied series of tortures,
that noble mother disregarded all of it because of her
25 faith in God. In the council chamber of her own
heart, so to speak, she saw clever advocates, nature
and parenthood and maternal love and the torment of
her
26 children - a mother holding two votes in regard to her
children, one to consign
27 them to death and the other to preserve them alive;
but she did not decide on the
28 safe course that would preserve her sons for a little
while , but like a true daughter
29 of God-fearing Abraham called to mind Abraham's
unflinching bravery. O mother of the nation, champion of the Law, defender of true religion, and win-
ner of the
30 prize in the inward contest of the heart! More noble

than men in fortitude and
31 stronger than heroes in endurance! Like the ark of
Noah, carrying the universe in the worldwide cata-
clysm and stoutly enduring the waves, so did you
guardian of the Law, buffeted on every side in the
flood of the passions and by the mighty gales of your
son's torments, so did you by your perseverance
nobly weather the storms that assailed you for religion's sake.

1 **16** If then a woman and indeed a woman of advance
years, the mother of seven sons, held out while looking upon her children being tortured to death, we
must
2 concede that devout reason is sovereign over the passions. I have therefore demonstrated that not only
ment have conquered human passions but that even a
3 woman despised the greatest torments. Not so wild
were the lions around Daniel nor so blazing hot in its
greedy flame was the furnace of Mishael[a] as the natural mother's love that burned in her when she saw
her seven sons so indiscriminately
4 tortured. Dan 6; Dan.3
But by pious reason the mother quenched all these
fiery emotions.
5 There is this too to consider, that if, as being a mother, the woman had been weak in spirit, she would
have wept over them and spoken perhaps as follows:
6 "Ah, thrice-wretched woman that I am, yes more
than thrice-wretched! I have
7 borne seven sons and am the mother of none! How
vain were these seven pregnancies, how futile these
seven times ten mouths[b] with child, how fruitless
8 the nursing and wretched the suckling! In vain, my
children, did I endure these
9 many pains for you and the even more severe strains
of rearing you. Alas for my sons, some unmarried,

others married but to no purpose! I shall never set
eyes on any children of yours nor shall I know the
happiness of being called grandmother.
10 Woe is me, who had many handsome children, but
am now bereft and all alone
11 with my many sorrows! Nor shall I have any of my
sons to bury me when I die."
12 But the holy and God-fearing mother lamented none
of them with any such dirge, nor urged any of them
to avoid death, nor grieved over them in the moment
13 of their death. Rather, as though she had a mind of
adamant and were this time bringing her brood of
sons'[c] to birth into immortal life, she encouraged
them and
14 pled with them to die for piety's sake. Mother, soldier
of God in piety's cause, elder and woman withal! By
your brave endurance you have overcome even the
15 tyrant and in deeds as in words have proven yourself
stronger than a man. When you were, seized along
with your sons, you stood watching Eleazar under
torture
16 and said to your children in the Hebrew tongue, "My
children, noble is the struggle, and since you have
been summoned to it to bear a witness for our nation,
17 fight zealously for our ancestral Law. Shameful
were it indeed that this old man should endure agonies for piety's sake, while you young men were ter-
rified of
18 torments. Remember that it is for God's sake you
were given a share in the world
19 and the benefit of life, and accordingly you owe it to
God to endure all hardship
20 for his sake, for whom our father Abraham ventured
boldly to sacrifice his son Isaac, the father of our
nation; and Isaac, seeing his father's hand, with knife
21 it, fall down against him, did not flinch. Gen 22:10
Daniel also, the righteous one, was thrown to the

lions, and Hananiah and Azariah and Mishael were
cast into the
22 fiery furnace, and all endured for the sake of God.
Dan 6; Dan 3
Therefore, you who have the
23 same faith in God must not be dismayed. For it
would be unreasonable for you who know true religion not to withstand hardships."
24 With these words the mother of the seven exhorted
each one and persuaded
25 them to die rather than transgress the commandment
of God, and they knew full well themselves that
those who die for the sake of God live unto God, as
do Abraham and Isaac and Jacob and all the patriarchs.[d] Ex 3:6; Mk 12:26F

1 **17** Some of the guards declared that when she, too,
was about to be seized and put to death, she threw
herself into the fire so that no one would touch her
body.[a] 2Mac 7:41
2 O mother with the seven sons, who broke down the
violence of the tyrant and
3 thwarted his wicked devices and exhibited the nobility of faith! Nobly set like a roof upon the pillars of
your children, you sustained, without yielding, the
4 earthquake of the tortures. Be of good cheer, therefore, mother of holy soul,
5 whose hope of endurance is secure with God. Not so
majestic stands the moon in heaven as you stand,
lighting the way to piety for your seven starlike sons,
6 honored by God and firmly set with them in heaven.
Job 39:9-40:5 For your childbearing was from our father
Abraham.

The effect of the martyrdoms

7 If it were possible for us to paint, as on a picture,[b]
the story of our piety, would not those who looked
upon it shudder to see the mother of seven sons endu-
ing
8 manifold torments unto death for piety's sake? It
would in fact be appropriate to inscribe upon their
tomb itself, as a memorial to those members of our
nation, the following words:

9 **HERE LIE BURIED AND AGED PRIEST**
AN OLD WOMAN
AND HER SEVEN SONS
THROUGH THE VIOLENCE OF A TYRANT
BENT ON DESTROYING THE POLITY OF
THE HEBREWS
10 **THEY VINDICATED THEIR RACE**
LOOKING UNTO GOD AND ENDURING
TORMENTS EVEN UNTO DEATH[c]

11 Truly divine was the contest in which they were
engaged. On that day virtue
12 was the umpire and the test to which they were put
was a test of endurance. The
13 prize for victory was incorruption in long-lasting life.
The first to enter the contest was Eleazar, but the
mother of the seven sons competed also, and the
brothers as
14 well took part. The tyrant was the adversary and the
world and the life of men
15 were the spectators. 1Cor 4:9
Piety won the victory and crowned her own contest-
ants.
16 Who did not marvel at the champions of the divine
Law; who were not amazed?
17. The tyrant himself and his whole council were

astonished at their endurance,
18 on account of which they now stand beside the divine
throne and live the life of
19 the age of blessing. For Moses says, *All the holy
ones are under you hands.*[d] Deut 33:3
20 These then, having consecrated themselves for the
sake of God, are now honored not only with this distinction but also by the fact that through them our
enemies
21 did not prevail against our nation, and the tyrant was
punished and our land purified, since they became, as
it were, a ransom for the sin of our nation.[e]
22 Though the blood of these righteous ones and
through the propitiation of their death the divine
providence rescued Israel, which had been shamefully treated.
23 For the tyrant Antiochus, observing intently their
heroism in virtue and their endurance under torture,
publicly held up their constancy as a model for his
24 soldiers and so roused them to such a high sense of
honor and such courage in infantry warfare and in the
siege of cities that he ravaged and overthrew all his
enemies.[f]

1 **18** O offspring of the seed of Abraham, children of
Israel, obey this Law and
2 be altogether true to your religion, knowing that
devout reason is master over the passions, and not
only over pains from within but also from outside
ourselves.[a]
3 Those men who surrendered their bodies to suffering
for piety's sake were in return not only admired by
mankind but were also deemed worthy of the divine
4 portion. And it was because of them that our nation
enjoyed peace - they revived
5 the observance of the Law in their land and repulsed

their enemies siege. And the tyrant Antiochus was punished on earth and continues to suffer punishment in death. For when he had failed absolutely to compel the people of Jerusalem to adopt the pagan way of life, and to forsake the customs of their fathers, he departed from Jerusalem and marched away against the Persians.

The mother's address to her children

6 The mother of the seven sons also addressed
these righteous saying to her children:
7 "I was a chaste maiden and did not leave my father's
house; but I kept guard
8 over the rib built into woman's body. Gen 2:22
No seducer of the desert nor deceiver in the field corrupted me, nor did the seducing and beguiling serpent defile my
9 maidenly purity.[c] Gen 3:1-7
Through all the days of my prime I stayed with my husband. When these sons[d] were grown up, their father died. Happy was he, for the life he lived was blessed with children, and he know not the pain of the time when
10 they were taken away. Gen 4:8
He, while he was still with you, taught you the Law and
11 the Prophets. Gen 22; Gen 39:7-23
He read to you of Abel, slain by Cain, of Isaac, offered as a burnt
12 offering, and of Joseph, in prison. Num 25:7-13
He spoke to you of the zeal of Phineas, and
13 taught you about Hananiah, Azariah, and Michael in
the fire. Dan 3:Dan 6
He sang the praises
14 of Daniel in the lions' den and called him blessed.
He reminded you of the scripture of Isaiah which

says, *Even though you walk through the fire, the flame*
15 *shall not burn you* Isa 43:2
He sang to you the psalm of David which says, *Many are*
16 *the afflictions of the righteous* Ps 34:19
He recited proverb of Solomon which says,
17 *He is a tree of life to those who do his will* Prov 3:18
He affirmed the word of Ezekiel,
18 *Shall these dry bones live?* Ezek 37:3
Nor did he forget the song that Moses taught which
19 says, *I kill and I make alive*, for this is your life and
the length[f] of your days, Deut 32:39
20 Ah! Bitter was the day and yet not bitter when
the cruel tyrant of the Greeks quenched[g] fire with fire
in his fierce braziers, and in a furious rage brought to
the catapult and back again to his tortures those
seven sons of the daughter of Abraham;
21 he pierced the pupils of their eyes, their tongues he
cut out, and slew them with
22 all kinds of torment. And for these acts the divine
justice has pursued and will
23 pursue the accursed tyrant. But the sons of Abraham,
together with their mother, who won the victor's
prize, are gathered together in the choir of their
fathers,[h] having received pure and deathless souls
from God, to whom be glory forever and ever, Amen.

WisSol 8:19

030821 300 26 60W